"Pastor Mike is a great frie[n]... 's
my privilege to pastor alon[g] ... h
God's favorite city, Seattle. I[n] ...ne shares
hard-earned, invaluable less[o]... ...is life. His faith—and
awesome sense of humor—will inspire you on your own adventure through life."

Judah Smith, lead pastor of The City Church,
New York Times bestselling author of *Jesus Is* ____.

"Such a practical, helpful book! Mike Howerton, my longtime friend, uses a basic task of parenting—teaching a child to ride a bike—as a launching point for life lessons that will deepen your walk with Jesus and inspire you to develop a more vibrant faith."

Kay Warren, author of *Choose Joy:
Because Happiness Isn't Enough*

"If you're looking to recapture the adventure of your faith and all the possibilities that emerge when you embrace it with passion, you can't afford to miss *The Ride of Your Life*. Mike is the real deal. He speaks from the center of his heart, and he'll get you to look at your relationship with God like you never have before. You're going to love this book!"

Les Parrott, PhD, #1 *New York Times*
bestselling author of *Love Talk*

"Life is a lot like learning to ride a bike, and Mike Howerton brilliantly draws out great insights from the Bible for riding well. I loved the creativity and simplicity in thinking about how to keep my own balance and how to get up when I fall. Through it all, Mike compassionately points to the God of second chances who is available to help us move forward. This is a great book to read and share!"

Jud Wilhite, senior pastor of Central Christian
Church, author of *The God of Yes*

"Sometimes the most important lesson isn't a new lesson. It's reapplying simple truths that are often lost in the busyness and clutter of life. I'm not going to lie: *The Ride of Your Life* is simple—so simple that it's profound and refreshing. No matter where we are on the journey of following Christ, Mike Howerton helps us rediscover the courage and joy we need to pursue the convictions that God has placed upon our hearts."

Eugene Cho, lead pastor of Quest Church Seattle,
author of *Overrated: Are We More in Love
with the Idea of Changing the World
Than Actually Changing the World?*

"Mike Howerton's *The Ride of Your Life* is wonderful—winsome, adventurous, wise, and practical—full of valuable life concepts with heartfelt stories that bring it to life! Reading it is as pleasant as a summer evening's bike ride."

Tom Flick, President of Tom Flick Communications,
Leadership Speaker for Kotter International

"Whether Mike Howerton is speaking or writing, I am leaning in. Rarely is there a new, fresh voice that speaks deeply to life, and Mike's is one of those. I found myself laughing hard, thinking deeply, and wanting to be different. I think you will too. Buckle up and enjoy the ride."

Doug Fields, bestselling author of *Refuel* and *Be Her
Hero: The One Your Wife Has Been Waiting For*

The Ride
of Your Life

The Ride

OF Your Life

What I Learned about God, Love, and Adventure by Teaching My Son to Ride a Bike

MIKE HOWERTON

BakerBooks
a division of Baker Publishing Group
Grand Rapids, Michigan

Published by Baker Books
a division of Baker Publishing Group
P.O. Box 6287, Grand Rapids, MI 49516-6287
www.bakerbooks.com

Printed in the United States of America

Library of Congress Cataloging-in-Publication Data is on file at the Library of
Congress, Washington, DC.

ISBN 978-0-8010-1392-8

Unless otherwise indicated, Scripture quotations are from the *Holy Bible*, New
Living Translation, copyright © 1996, 2004, 2007 by Tyndale House Foundation.
Used by permission of Tyndale House Publishers, Inc., Carol Stream, Illinois
60188. All rights reserved.

Scripture quotations labeled Message are from *The Message* by Eugene H. Peterson, copyright © 1993, 1994, 1995, 2000, 2001, 2002. Used by permission of
NavPress Publishing Group. All rights reserved.

Scripture quotations labeled NIV are from the Holy Bible, New International
Version®. NIV®. Copyright © 1973, 1978, 1984, 2011 by Biblica, Inc.™ Used
by permission of Zondervan. All rights reserved worldwide. www.zondervan.com

To protect the privacy of some individuals, some names and details have been
changed.

14 15 16 17 18 19 20   7 6 5 4 3 2 1

I dedicate this book to the fine people of Overlake Christian Church. You are truly the best church family I know at making the most radical difference in this world and building a beautiful culture of worship balanced by outlandish love. You make this a great place to be on the journey and an incredible place to raise my family, and I love you. Thank you for taking this ride with me.

Contents

Contents

Vignette

I have a five-year-old friend named Lola.

Last week she learned to ride her bike, mastering the principles found in this book.

Her dad, one of my best friends, showed me a picture he took of her after she learned to ride.

Her shock of red hair is a bit tangled, messy with summer sunshine and sweat. She is sitting so that both her knees and her elbows are visible, and all are sporting fresh battle wounds: raspberries and grass stains.

But her smile radiates. There is no hint of grief over her skinned knees hidden in her expression. Her eyes are steadfast with self-assurance. And I see joy. Not the shallow, flippant joy that comes from some passing novelty. She has put the training wheels away for good. Forevermore, she's a joyful rider of the bicycle.

Lola's is the hard-fought joy that comes from overcoming and expanding her world.

Maybe it's been a while. But it's high time for you to experience that joy again.

Introduction

When the spirits are low, when the day appears dark, when work becomes monotonous, when hope hardly seems worth having, just mount a bicycle and go out for a spin down the road, without thought on anything but the ride you are taking.

Sir Arthur Conan Doyle

It came to a boiling point one summer afternoon.

I pulled my car in the driveway after work, just in time to witness my son hurling his bike to the ground in frustration, his face red and tearful. If I couldn't already read it clearly in my wife's expression, she spelled it out for me: "He's *your* son," she said through clenched teeth. "*You* need to teach him to ride this bike." Then she turned and left, the bike jumbled at an odd angle but dominating the scene like a talisman of failure, a metal sculpture askew with defeat.

"Caleb, buddy, come over here." I knelt down to his level.

He picked up his bike and walked slowly over. My mind was racing. I shot up a silent prayer. And suddenly, miraculously, I knew how I needed to approach his instruction.

"Caleb," I said, "I'll teach you how to ride your bike. No problem at all." (I was curious to hear where I was heading with this.)

"It will take five days." (Five? Where in the world did I get five?)

"Each day I'll teach you one lesson, and we'll practice together. By the weekend, you'll be the Jedi Master of the two-wheeled set." (I was inspired from on high and the poetry was beginning to flow.)

"The neighbor kids will rise up and call you blessed. Does that sound good?"

He nodded his head, wiped the tears from his eyes. "Okay, Dad." The boy was game.

Earnest but with compassion, I said, "Son, we will focus hard on each lesson for twenty minutes. But when Daddy says the lesson is over, it's over. We give each other high fives, put the bike in the garage, and go inside to drink lemonade. Deal?" I extended my hand. With wide eyes he soulfully, sincerely shook my hand. He wanted this badly. He was ready to believe.

And so it began.

Each of the five days, we learned one lesson. We practiced, and we were done in twenty minutes as planned. The trainings were in a specific order, and each lesson provided the foundation for the next. Each day we reviewed the previous instructions. But, most important, we focused on one teaching at a time.

By the end of the five days, Caleb was in fact riding his bike around like a fury, a Yoda on wheels. He was having an absolute blast, going from frustration to freedom. He overcame. His universe expanded. His horizon lengthened. He was ready for all the adventure a master of the art of cycling could handle.

The lessons were simple and intuitive:

Lesson one: No fear

Lesson two: Balance

Lesson three: Steering

Lesson four: Braking

Lesson five: Starting from a standstill

The last lesson would display mastery of all of the previous lessons, because it would force Caleb to create his own momentum, often after a fall.

Since this experience I've realized that these five lessons aren't just for learning to ride a bike; they're for mastering any new challenge, for doing life well. They will help when facing the rigors of junior high or heading off to college; they're for starting a business, planting a church, beginning a marriage or prizing it for the long haul, playing an instrument, coaching a team, planning a road trip, or learning to surf. In other words, it turns out that these principles are virtually universal.

Childhood is quite often about embracing these five lessons in order to enjoy a new skill and the new paradigm that skill provides. Adulthood seems to force many of us into a mold where we just hunker down and hold on. We find ourselves not interested in learning any new skill, mastering any new concept, or tackling any new horizon. Our paradigm gets old and boring. We forget that life is for *living.* We forget we were made to live as overcomers.

So here is the challenge: What new bicycle do you need to learn how to ride?

What is the new paradigm that you wish you could break into but haven't been able to? Is there a language you need to learn? A service trip to a third-world country you've been dreaming about taking? A book within you that you need to write? A career shift you need to make? Art within you that needs to be created? A person you need to ask out for coffee?

Maybe you can articulate the desire, but you have no idea how to start.

Start here. Start with these five lessons.

With these lessons I discovered a process, and the system bred success for Caleb. But there was something grander and more glorious going on. I believe that God revealed his invitation to abundant living. This is a process for sucking the marrow out of life, for enjoying the fullest amount of love and adventure. I've seen these principles bear much fruit in my own life and in the lives of those I've had the privilege of journeying with, and I offer them humbly now to you.

Remember the LORD your God. He is the one who gives you power to be successful. (Deut. 8:18)

Lesson One

No Fear

Arguing with Fear

When a resolute young fellow steps up to the great bully, the world, and takes him boldly by the beard, he is often surprised to find it comes off in his hand, and that it was only tied on to scare away the timid adventurers.

Ralph Waldo Emerson

I worked together with my wife, Jodie, to teach our oldest child, Alexandra, to ride her bike. We gave it our best, chaotic, scattershot teaching effort, and she caught on fairly quickly. There were a few spills and tears and some laughter, and then she was off and riding. She got it. She overcame. Her universe grew.

When Jodie began teaching our son, Caleb, he was overwhelmed by the sheer number of things to keep in mind. He was frustrated, and he vented his frustration at his mom. But I sensed this was because of an underlying tension: he was afraid.

Getting Going

The first lesson Caleb needed to learn was not to fear. He needed to have it branded on his little heart: *Do not be afraid.* Much of his frustration was simply the product of how unsettled he felt.

I had Caleb run inside and wash the tears off, grab a quick snack, and then meet me back on the yard next to our driveway.

"Buddy, are you ready?" I asked.

He nodded somberly; there was a steely glint in his eyes.

"The first lesson is no fear. Can you say, 'no fear'?"

"No fear," he repeated.

"Fear has no place in learning to ride. Together we are going to banish fear. We are going to stomp it out. There is no room in your courageous heart for even the tiniest bit of fear. Okay?"

"Okay, Dad," he said, because he knew I wanted him to. "But what if I fall?"

"At some point, you might fall. So kneel down here."

We both dropped down and felt the grass with our hands.

"Look, the grass on our lawn is soft. Even if you do fall, it's not going to hurt."

He didn't look too sure.

"But Caleb, listen." I gently placed my hands on his shoulders. "Today's lesson is about having no fear. So today, I promise you, you have nothing to fear whatsoever. And the reason you don't have anything to fear is because I'm going to be holding your seat the entire time. You don't have anything to be afraid of, because I love you, I will be holding you, and I will not let you go. Okay?"

His face softened. "Okay," he said, and this time he meant it.

We spent the next twenty minutes with Caleb riding his bike in the yard while I was running alongside him, holding his seat the whole time. He gained confidence, and he began to trust himself, even to trust that the yard was safe to fall on, but we didn't focus on any of those things. I only wanted him to be encouraged, to have energy to continue his training, and to have no fear.

"What's lesson one?" I'd pant out, running beside him.

"No fear!"

"How come?"

"Because you've got me!"

"That's right," I'd say. "Your dad has you. Don't forget it! And I love you, and I'm not going to let you fall." And the whole time I was holding his seat, running and winded and thinking, *Gee, I've really got to get in shape.*

The Problem with Fear

We need to learn this lesson too. God has us. He loves us. And he's not going to let us fall. One of the most important reasons we must learn the lesson is because of the damage fear does to us. It's an assault against our identity as loved children of our heavenly Father. Wreaking havoc upon our potential, fear attacks the full life God has for us.

I have a friend who doesn't believe in God, but I know she believes this truth. She tells me things like, "The universe is conspiring to help me." She'll tell me a story about how she was "thinking good thoughts" about a situation that she was nervous to confront, and then when she entered that situation, it was as if the solution presented itself. She wants to be grateful, but she doesn't know who to thank. So she "gives it back out" to the universe.

When we talk, I affirm her journey and her fearless approach. I do believe that the universe operates by certain guidelines, I tell her, and I do believe there is a conspiracy in her favor. And I suggest to her, "Maybe behind the whole thing there is a Somebody. And just maybe, maybe that Somebody loves you." For me, God's love provides the reason to live fearlessly.

Fear erects a ceiling limiting our lives. Fear controls us by telling us what we can and cannot do. Fear chains us to the floor and prevents us from soaring. Fear prevents us from trying to master a new skill. It talks us out of taking the first step. Fear prevents us from loving, hoping, believing. Fear is an assault on our joy. It is what keeps us from allowing God to lead us into a new day, and it's what was keeping Caleb from learning to ride. That's why we had to start here.

Living in fear is a kind of death, which is why there is something so very powerful about stepping through fear. Stepping through our fear destroys it. On the other side of fear we experience life—heart-pounding, chills-inducing life. Besides, the alternative is a bummer.

Fear Begets Regrets

When I was in high school, I played football and drove a fire-engine red '66 Mustang with thick chrome rims. I kept this car clean—washed, toweled, waxed, and shining. I kept a full bottle of Armor All in the trunk. "You are *way* cool," I would tell myself as I drove, to hide my insecurity about keeping a full bottle of Armor All in my trunk. Most days when I drove to school, I'd drive down the hill, out of my way, so I could drive past Sofia's house.

Sofia drove a red Pontiac Fiero. She was on the swim team. She was tan. She had a great smile. So I'd drive past her house day after day after day. I'd daydream that she would come outside to get in her car just as I was driving by, and I'd stop, and we'd chat.

Occasionally I actually would see her coming out to get into her car as I was driving by. It terrified me. I drove faster. I never stopped to talk with her. I desperately wanted to, but I didn't have a single conversation with her. Not one. I didn't even know if she knew my name, and I imagined it'd be weird stopping and making up stuff to talk about. In my fear, I imagined it'd go something like, "Hi, Sofia. I'm Mike. How's it going? I'm on my way to school too. Yeah, I go this way." I'd squint like Eastwood and gaze significantly into the middle distance. "It takes longer, but I get there faster. You know what I mean? We both have red cars. I gotta go." And with images of crashing and burning in my mind, I'd just keep driving by, silently, day after day after day.

At my twenty-year high school reunion, I saw Sofia again and met her husband. Both were triathletes, successful, funny, and living on the East Coast. But when she saw me, she grabbed her husband and said to him (I'm embarrassed to write this), "Babe, this is that guy in high school I was telling you about! He's the one who drove that cool Mustang! Mike, you drove by my house all the time and I was always hoping you'd stop to talk!"

D'oh. True story. Cue the forehead slap.

Now I love my life. I'm head over heels about my godly, talented wife, and my kiddos are my favorite humans on the planet, so this tale isn't a gripe or a wistful I-want-to-do-my-life-over moment. It's simply a reminder that there are others who are wishing we'd step through fear as well. My dad has always told me that we regret the things we didn't try more than the things we were bold enough to attempt.

A Scary Encounter

By the way, my dad was in the US Marines. He's one of those barrel-chested, dismember-you-ten-ways-with-a-paper-clip kind of guys. When he wasn't shipped out on assignment, he'd get home in the late afternoon, and we'd often play catch or wrestle. So there were many days I'd be waiting excitedly for him at the end of the day. One evening I heard his car pull into the driveway, and I made a quick plan to start a hide-and-seek game before he got in the door.

My plan was to hide in the garage and call my dad to come find me. Understand, our garage looked like an M. C. Escher painting of a junkyard inside an antique store inside a junkyard. I had found the perfect hiding spot, on the back side of the love seat, behind the stack of old John Denver vinyls, underneath some hanging tools, and inside an empty cupboard. Without some kind of magic wand, it'd take him forever to find me.

I had left the light on, and when I heard him come into the house, I called, "Dad, I'm in the garage, come and find me!" Then I scurried into my hiding place inside of the cabinet. I heard the door to the garage creak open, then shut, with the light turned off. My dad hadn't heard me! He'd just peeked in the garage, not seen anyone, switched off the light, and shut the door. I was left alone, in the pitch darkness, shut up inside a cupboard, in the far end of the junkyard that was my garage.

He'll come back. He's coming back. He's got to come back, I thought. I waited.

And waited.

And waited.

And waited.

For, like, thirty whole seconds.

Then I decided that I was going to have to handle this one. I could make it out of this black hole on my own. I slid open the cabinet door, cautiously. I leaned forward and sat still. I made no noise. I wasn't even breathing.

Someone else was.

As I froze in complete silence, I could hear a soft rustle. A muted breathing. Someone was in the garage with me! The horror of this thought made the hair on the back of my neck stand on end. These were the days when a man affectionately known as the "Night Stalker" was terrorizing Southern California, causing my brother and sister and me to sleep in the same room. One night he had shown up in my town of Mission Viejo, and now it was obvious he was in my garage. Why oh why had I decided to hide in the bottomless pit of my dark garage with a serial killer? I'd never be seen again! If only my dad had come to find me, with the light on like it was supposed to be, this never would have happened.

I was still sitting in terrified silence, but I knew I had to make a run for it. I had to scramble for the slit of light that was barely showing under the garage door. That was my beacon of safety. With a deep breath, I plunged out from my hole, crashed into the stacks of vinyls, vaulted the love seat, barked my shin against a toolbox, and in a single bound made it across the floor littered with bikes, grabbed the doorknob of the garage door, and pulled it open, my shaking frame flooded with warm light. From this place of safety, I turned back toward the garage, when from the depths of blackness a figure jumped at me and shouted, "Boo!" It was my dad.

I wet myself.

You know that old saying, "You have nothing to fear but fear itself"? That guy didn't have a dad in the military who terrified him in a dark garage. Sometimes there is something to fear. Sometimes the thing you dread actually happens. Sometimes the worst thing possible is what impossibly happens. But even then you find that God has been holding you the whole time. In fact, the only purpose fear might serve is to cause us to cling to the Father. When we call to him, he takes our fear away.

The reason Caleb didn't need to be afraid when he was learning to ride is that I had him. I was holding him. The reason you don't need to be afraid is that God has you. The Lord is holding you. The Lord loves you.

The Somebody who crafted the universe will never let you go.

And he doesn't get winded.

Risky Business

Often the difference between a successful person and a failure
is not one's better abilities or ideas, but the courage that one
has to bet on one's ideas, to take a calculated risk, and to act.

André Malraux

Caleb was incredibly frustrated before he could learn to ride
his bike. Jodie had been trying to teach him, but there were too
many things for Caleb to keep in mind, and the night before
we started our lessons he was whining. "This is impossible!" he
said. I tried to offer him encouragement, but he was so unsure
of himself, he couldn't hear me. He was having trouble believing that the risk would be worth the reward.

"Caleb," I gently said, "you can do it."

"Dad, I can't."

"Son, you can. I'm not guessing. I know this."

"How do you know?"

I said, "Buddy, I've done it. And I know you. You're strong
and athletic and you have good balance and coordination. Not

only that, but everyone I've ever seen who tries to ride a bike ends up riding a bike. I'm not pretending I know your future, dude—I know it. You will learn how to ride your bike."

And I meant it. I wasn't offering this as a form of pressure, and I wasn't just blowing sunshine. I was offering it as a type of solid reassurance. I had no doubt whatsoever for his journey ahead, because I knew exactly where it would end: in his total mastery of this currently daunting reality. I didn't think for a nanosecond that it was impossible for him. Because it wasn't.

Now, imagine that riding a bike is a metaphor for something you're trying to master. What is that for you? Reaching your sales goals, opening a new business, getting your graduate degree, or beginning a dating relationship? Maybe you take this personally into your marriage or into raising your kids. Maybe you are at the very beginning of understanding your faith journey and stepping into a relationship with God. But imagine that God has your seat, that he's running alongside of you and saying, "You can do it." And you're responding through the lens of fear, like Caleb. You're saying, "No, I can't." And then it starts to dawn on you—your heavenly Father really does have you. Almighty God really is holding you. And he's not guessing you can. He's not hoping. He knows you and what you're made of because you're uniquely made in his image and reflect his glory as only you can. So, without any reservation whatsoever, he responds, "Yes, you can."

Trusting God looks to us like risky business.

But God knows he's a sure thing.

I struggle here often.

Enemy Assaults

It doesn't help that we have an enemy who loves to assault our identity as God's dearly loved children and use our fears as a weapon against us. It's the quiet whisper of hell: "Admit it, you can't." I get this faint whisper all the time. I hear it playing on an old scratchy phonograph in my mind: "You'll realize you can't write and give the whole thing up. You can't lead a church. Look at you—you're barely a Christian some days, let alone a leader. Look at that guy there—he's a *real* pastor, so why don't you give it up?" And I'm sure you've heard the whispers as well: "You can't be a husband, wife, father, mother, leader, volunteer, or a successful (fill-in-the-blank)."

I don't know what the whisper aims at in your life. Whatever it is, I want you to hear me say, "It is a lie." You need to say it too.

Instead, listen to your Father. Listen to the One who loves you, who knows you, who is holding you.

"You can do this."

Even your heart might betray you and join in with the lie, and your insecurities might sing in chorus. So don't listen to my words. Listen to your Father's. He's saying, "You can. I know it. I know where we're going. Let's go there together."

Risking Bravery

One of the riskiest things I ever did was confront an unknown intruder.

During my years in college, I spent a summer sleeping on the floor of a small second-story apartment in Venice Beach with four other Pepperdine roommates. Venice is a wonderful freak show, and I love it dearly, with its street performers and bodybuilders and turbaned Rollerbladers gliding through fresh sea air trailing vapors of hemp. Venice also boasts less than adequate parking, and it does enjoy a good bit of crime. So there is that.

Three of my buddies and I had come home late one night, and we noticed there was an unknown car parked in our apartment's only parking spot. As we walked upstairs, we realized the front door was ajar, and the lights were off.

I called out, "Hello?"

Nobody answered, but I could hear something in the back bedroom. I walked shakily to the bedroom door, turned the knob, and began to open the door, when it suddenly slammed shut, then locked. Somebody was there! I've honestly never been more terrified in my life. My buddy hurriedly called 911, and I, not knowing what else to do, took my belt off to hold like some sort of weapon of parental discipline, and I began to scream, with all the veins in my neck pulsing, at the door.

"I don't know who you are, but we've called the cops! If you come out, we're going to pound you! But if you stay there, you're going to get arrested!" At least that's what I wanted to yell.

My heart was pounding so hard, my nerves were so on edge, what I actually yelled was more like, "Uggaaaggghhh-cops!" After an uncomfortable standoff with a silent door, the door-knob turned slowly. The door opened. It was our fifth room-mate, looking sheepish.

His girlfriend had brought him home. It was her car in the parking spot. They were sort of making out, so they didn't want me to open the door, and that's why they slammed and locked it. "Oh," I said, relieved, deflated. "Sorry. Can we apologize to her?" I asked, kind of horrified.

"No," he said. "She's not here anymore. She got so scared when you called the cops that she jumped out the window and drove home." The bicycle cop who showed up thought it was funny, but it took me a long time to stop trembling and relax after my brush with bravery. Or something.

The riskiest confrontation of my life turned out not to be risky at all. Just a roommate and a misunderstanding. And I would argue that most of the "risks" we take, in hindsight, turn out to be very similar.

Risking Comfort

Now, it's important to note that *uncomfortable* does not equal *negative*. *Uncomfortable* merely means "not comfortable." I wonder how often in our lives we shy away from uncomfortable, when stepping through our discomfort could lead to the new adventure Jesus is prompting us to pursue.

Embracing the *no fear* lesson doesn't mean that you pretend you lack an emotional response to life's challenges. It doesn't mean you pretend *uncomfortable* away. It simply means you look fear in the eye and step forward anyway.

When you're stepping through fear and taking a risk, it's good to remember that you're never alone.

Jump

One sunny morning, I jumped out of a perfectly good airplane for a sermon illustration. I get light-headed just thinking about it. When I jumped from the plane, I was doing what is called a tandem jump. I was connected at the hip and shoulderblades with Todd, an expert. Todd had logged over five thousand jumps. He was going to make sure we were jumping in the right location. He was going to make sure that our equipment was more than sufficient. He was going to pull the chute at the right time. He was the expert, and he talked me through things, step-by-step.

The adventure of jumping out of a plane clicked into Todd's harness has to be one of the biggest adrenaline surges of my entire life. There was glory and rush as every cell in my body did cartwheels while my sinus cavities attempted to swallow my eyeballs.

I'm so glad I did it.

I never want to do it again.

When I talk about obeying and walking with God, I'm talking about clicking into his harness. I'm talking about stepping through your fear and jumping—not away from God but with him. Place yourself into the mighty, loving hands of the One who loves you most. Trust him. Obey him. Walk with him. He's got you. He's holding your heart.

Confidence, joy, security—these are the blessings that come with God's companionship. You will find that he is enough, that his presence will carry you through an uncomfortable season. You will find that he can land you safely, even when the whole thing looks like risky business.

> My flesh and my heart may fail,
>   but God is the strength of my heart
>   and my portion forever. (Ps. 73:26 NIV)

3

Bigger and Better

Courage is not the absence of fear, but rather the judgment that something else is more important than fear.

James Neil Hollingworth

When I learned to ride my bike, I was a first grader in Orange County, California. I had washed cars in my neighborhood (going door-to-door with a bucket, a sponge, and puppy-dog eyes) in order to save up half the money it took to buy my first bike. It was a beauty: a shiny, black, banana-seated, flag-on-the-back, cards-stuck-in-the-spokes Schwinn. (When I told my kids I wanted this book to be called *How to Schwinn in Life*, they thought I had entered a region known as Epic Lame.)

My buddy Scott and I headed down the sidewalk on Muir-lands Parkway, past the orange groves (this was back when Orange County lived up to its name), and rode all the way to the donut shop on El Toro Road. This was no mere ride. It was a quest (1.2 miles!). There was a Donkey Kong game at the donut shop and a Carl's Jr. next door, which was a huge payoff. In my world of kid-dom, this was the pinnacle of existence, and it opened up to me only after my bike-riding skills were mastered. When my paradigm expanded, this adventure was suddenly added to my universe.

When you learned to ride your bike, you embraced a massive paradigm shift as well, so that although you were simply acquiring a new skill, the end result was that your world grew bigger and better in the process. Do you remember what friends you could now visit with your new travel radius? Do you remember what adventures were now possible, what trails were there to be explored, what delights were suddenly within grasp? No longer would you merely stroll down a hill—now you were free to *fly*!

The Bionic Man

My buddy Ed told me he used to be a drug dealer/hell-raiser while he was in his motorcycle gang. At thirty-six years old, he found himself in federal prison with one leg gone due to a drunken motorcycle accident, when a pastor visited him in jail. The pastor loved Ed and called him out, telling him he was just playing a stupid game with his life. Then he asked, "How's that working out for you?" Ed realized it wasn't working out for him at all. He prayed and gave his life to Jesus. Now he tells people, "I got me some jailhouse religion, and I'm holding on to it!"

Since trading up, Ed has continued to walk a road that is bigger and better. He earned an associate's degree in prison and landed a great job at Microsoft and moved to Seattle. God brought an amazing woman into his life, Linda, and they got married. As they were starting their life together as a married couple, Ed realized they needed to give God their debt, and God helped them get their finances in order. And then

Ed recognized his health and weight were moving in a bad direction. So he offered his body to God, and his faith helped him get his fitness in order. Ed just kept trading his plans for God's plans, which were bigger and better, all along the way. Last summer, with the help of multiple prosthetic legs, Ed was able to complete his first Ironman triathlon.

Ed told me, "As we traded up, the adventure just kept getting bigger and better." He told our church family, "It's never too late to change. It's never too late to go bigger with your life, to go bigger with your faith, to go bigger with your impact. God loves you, and he wants to do infinitely more than we can ask or imagine through us."

When we introduced Ed to our church family, he brought all of his legs. He's got them for multiple purposes: swimming, running, biking, and so on. Surveying all those legs in awe, one of the kids told him, "I've never had a bionic friend before!"

When God's got us covered, we can trade up in a big way.

Fear Whispers

You've written something off in your life, thinking, "Well, that's just the way it is," or "That's just the way I am." And so it's a bit of a risk to trade up for something better; you're afraid to go bigger because you're afraid of disappointment. You're afraid that you'll end up back where you started. In fact, some of you are writing this chapter off already. You're thinking, "I've heard this message before. It doesn't work."

There is an enemy of your soul who earnestly wants this chapter to be called "Face it, you'll fail," which is a lie from the pit of hell. This is why we must reject his voice whenever we hear it. When we lean into the presence of our loving Savior and listen to the voice of our King and Friend, with his help we embrace the challenge. We are ready for the adventure. In faith, joy, and power, we are offered more. In freedom, healing, and wholeness, we can go bigger.

There is nothing to be afraid of, because our Father holds us and loves us.

No matter how big you think God is, he is bigger still, and he invites us to enter into the magnitude of his largesse. He invites us to participate more fully in his greatness. It's all there for us. And yet many of us, much of the time, live lives far below the levels of joy and peace and love and grace that Christ died on the cross to purchase for us. We neglect to claim the spiritual strength that is ours. In our attempts to live fearlessly, it is so important that we remind ourselves that our courage comes from our Father.

How It Can Look

At the beginning of the summer, our church's student ministries had an activity where they went out in teams and played a game called Bigger and Better. The idea is that your team starts with a paper clip, and then you go door-to-door and explain to folks that you're a part of a scavenger hunt–style game, and you're looking to trade your paper clip for something bigger and better. Now, it's important to realize that these trade-ups actually happened. Every team was able to come back with something much more complex, more expensive, and much larger than a paper clip. The only thing each team had when the game started was a paper clip and a dream.

Team 1 started with a paper clip, which they traded for a plastic inflatable pool, which then went for a Dean Martin poster, which was traded for a case of Mountain Dew, which made way for an Xbox video game controller, which was swapped for a used washer and dryer set, which were both given in exchange for a brand-new laptop computer. Each trade was bigger and incredibly better.

Even more unbelievable was Team 2, which also began with a paper clip, which they were able to trade for a liter of 7UP, which then went for a garden gnome, which was transformed into a Zune MP3 player and then ultimately swapped for a functioning John Deere tractor! I find this amazing. Not that our students knew what a Zune was, but that each trade was such an obvious *trade-up*.

This is the kind of trade-up some of us need to experience in our faith.

We come to God where we are, and he takes us higher. We give God our worry and trade up for his peace. We give God life on our own strength, and he gives us life by his strength. We give him our life of isolation, and he gives us a life of friendship. We give him our life of selfishness, and he gives us a life of generosity. We give him our life of sin, and he gives us a life of freedom. We give him our life of confusion, and he gives us a life of purpose. We give him our life of dissatisfaction, and he gives us a life of joy.

These are good trades.

No matter where we are in the journey, it's time to trade up. No matter how far you've come, there's greater distance to travel. No matter how much love you've experienced from God, there is deeper love to delve. No matter how much victory you've enjoyed, there is more!

Allow God to love you.

Trust him with the fears that you need to step through.

Trade up for the adventure he has in mind for you, which will always be bigger and better than what you could come up with on your own.

4

Off We Go

Here is the world. Beautiful and terrible things will happen.
Do not be afraid.

Frederick Buechner

Last night my dreams took a nightmarish turn. Something
about a gang of serial-killing, tuxedo-wearing babies and a kit-
ten with fangs of doom. I woke up in a cold sweat and listened
intensely to the silence of 2:22 a.m.

Only it wasn't silent. I thought I heard a small noise in the
hall.

It was nothing, right? But there it was again. Now I was
sure of it. I started praying the blood of Jesus over my family
and was about ready to open up a banshee howl and leap from
my covers like a terrified ninja when I saw the outline of my
daughter in the door frame.

"Dad, I can't sleep. Can you tuck me in and pray for me?"

So that one turned out okay, as most nightmares do.

God meets us again and again, and it turns out that even on the occasion when the worst happens, he is there. He has you. But the overwhelming majority of time, the worst never happens. Fear fades like a nightmare in the light of the noonday sun. A vast multitude of our worries evaporate like the dew on the morning grass. This is why Jesus tells us not to worry. He knows it doesn't make sense. He sees it doesn't help us make progress.

Bold

God begins so many human interactions with this message: *Do not be afraid.* Again and again the first words that are offered when an agent of the divine shows up on the scene are the words "Fear not!" There are a couple of reasons for this.

The first is that whenever God sends even his least impressive messenger, the sheer weight-of-glory factor is so great that it leaves mere mortals facedown in the dirt wishing they'd worn their Depends. We can't handle being in the presence of those who stand in the presence of God. The reality of how far short we fall is suddenly revealed to us. The full weight of our sin and broken humanity is illuminated when we stand in the presence of perfection. God knows all of this, so he's instructed his angels to begin every interaction with us with the words "Fear not!" It's heaven's standing policy.

Fear is our first response, so assurance is the Lord's.

The second reason is that God knows that when fear grips us, it limits us and keeps us in bondage. Fear prevents us from seeing a larger picture. Fear prevents us from trusting that God will be God. Fear keeps us in chains so that we don't behave, act, or decide to walk in faith. Even our imagined fear (and most of it is imagined) has an impact on the way we live.

I was listening to a radio program called *This American Life,* and the host, Ira Glass, was talking about an experiment done with children on the behavioral impact imagination has. Each individual child would enter a bare room with the instructor, who was holding an open, visibly empty box. The instructor talked to the child about how there was no such thing as magic and how our imaginations could not suddenly make things appear. All of the children, one by one, agreed. Then the instructor closed the box lid and asked each child to imagine something. Half of the children were instructed to imagine it was magically filled with cookies. The instructor would ask follow-up questions like, "How many cookies do you imagine are in this box? What kind of cookies do you imagine are inside? Can you imagine how good these cookies taste?"

The other group of kids was asked to imagine the box was suddenly filled with snakes. The follow-up questions to these were similar: "How many snakes do you imagine are inside of the box? What kinds of snakes are they? Can you picture in your mind whether these snakes are poisonous or not?" After this exercise in imagination, the instructor would once again remind each child that our imaginations can't make things real and the box was empty. But he kept the lid on the box. And then the instructor would make an excuse to leave the room for a moment.

The child was left alone in the room with nothing but the closed box sitting on a table. Every single child who imagined that the box was filled with cookies opened the box when left alone, just to see if maybe by some chance the delicious cookies they had imagined suddenly appeared. Each kid who imagined the box filled with snakes, when left alone, crept slowly away from the box; not a single one of them opened it.

Our fears, even imagined, really do have a negative impact on the way we live.

This kind of fear comes from somewhere. It comes from our limitations, our brokenness, our enemy. Fear can come from a number of sources but never comes from our Father.

Some of our fear is learned behavior because we've been hurt. We've been injured—by others or by ourselves. We touch the hot stove as a toddler, and we have a healthy fear of touching the hot stove in the future, but what if we refused to ever enter a kitchen again? We have to lean into our Father, asking him to help us understand which fear is healthy self-protection and which is nonsense, needlessly stealing our freedom, healing, and wholeness.

Our Father loves us. Perfectly. His sort of comprehensive, unending love banishes fear.

"There Is No Pain; There Is Only Joy"

When my buddy Jay and I ran the Portland marathon, we both hit our personal best. Something about the energy of the day and the strength we drew from one another along the road made both of us feel extra fueled as we delighted to punish our bodies relentlessly for three-plus hours. One of the ways we encouraged one another was by repeating a line that had popped into my head, "There is no pain; there is only joy." And we had some time to unpack this, so we did a bit. We talked about how good it was to be in Portland together. We talked about how thankful we were that the course route didn't have much elevation change. We spoke about the blessing of being healthy and strong enough in our forties to be running this marathon. We reminded ourselves that we had plenty to be joyful about. We used this saying when Jay's digestion went south after an electrolyte gummy bear. We used this saying when my calf muscles threatened to seize up during the last few quivering miles. There is no pain; there is only joy. And when we finished our race, we celebrated together with our families, and the pain faded away into a distant memory. The joy became much more tangible.

Jesus kept his eyes on joy, and it carried him through the shame and pain of the cross. James tells us we need to consider even the trials we slog through as an opportunity for great joy. The promise of Scripture is that we will have trouble in this world, and when it comes we can remember that Jesus has overcome this world, and we are to live as joyful overcomers as well.

Strong Enough

I didn't promise Caleb he would never crash on his bike. I didn't promise he would never, ever get hurt if he learned to ride. I promised him that as he learned I'd hold him, and I wouldn't let him fall. But how long did Caleb expect me to run beside his bike holding the seat? Forever? Did Caleb imagine that when he became a teenager, he'd head out with his BMX bike to the jumps with his buddies while I ran beside him holding the seat? Of course not. We had an unspoken agreement. I would hold his seat only until he was ready for me to let go.

This is important because God is our loving Father. As our Father, he holds us until we are ready, until we are strong enough. Then off we go.

I recently went through a season with braces on my teeth. My teeth were behaving like fans at an open-seat Nirvana concert, all crowding forward and throwing punches. So for eighteen months I walked the road of braces with the world's nicest orthodontist. When he finally removed the braces, I asked him if I could keep them. It was the only time he'd received that request. He sealed them in a plastic bag and asked me what I wanted to do with them. "Nothing," I said. "I just want them to remind me that the point of braces is not to live with braces. The point of braces is to live with healthy teeth."

Training wheels on a bike are similar. The point of training wheels is to remove them once training has occurred. It is a form of designed obsolescence. In some ways I believe this is what God had in mind all along with the law he gave Israel. The point of the law wasn't the law. The point was to create a people who would no longer need it.

God holds us until we are strong, but the point of our Father's care is not to keep us from facing anything difficult in this life. The point of his care is to make us strong and healthy so we can flourish no matter what we face.

The implications for this truth are profound. If you find yourself in the midst of trouble, trial, or temptation, you can be absolutely certain of three things.

First, God is right next to you. He has not left your side. Even though he may no longer be holding the seat of your bicycle, he will never leave you.

Second, the only reason you're going through this difficulty is because your gracious, wise, and loving heavenly Father knows you are strong enough. You can do this.

Third, any fear you have can be cast into the presence of his perfect love.

> The LORD himself watches over you!
>> The LORD stands beside you as your protective
>> shade.
> The sun will not harm you by day,
>> nor the moon at night.
>
> The LORD keeps you from all harm
>> and watches over your life.
> The LORD keeps watch over you as you come and go,
>> both now and forever. (Ps. 121:5–8)

Lesson Two

Balance

5

How It Is with Balance

Life is like riding a bicycle. To keep your balance you must keep moving.

Albert Einstein

When Caleb and I went out on the second day, he was bubbling with excitement, talking about how he banished fear and how he knew he didn't have anything to worry about and, "Isn't it just *fun* to ride a bike, Dad?"

"It *is* fun, buddy," I said, "and that's the whole point, but it also takes some work, doesn't it? You have to keep lesson one in mind. Do you remember what it is?"

He yelled out, "No fear!"

"Good job. That's right. Banish fear from your heart. And do you remember why you don't need to be afraid?"

"Because my dad is *holding me*!" Caleb's never had trouble with volume.

"That's right. I've got you. I'm with you. So that means you're prepared for lesson two. Are you ready? Lesson two is simple: balance."

I put Caleb on his bike, and I held the seat stationary.

"Caleb, how hard do you think it would be to balance this bike while it is absolutely still?" He was wiggling and turning the handlebars spasmodically. "Hard, right? Only a very few people can balance on a bike when it's still, but I'm going to tell you the secret of balance, and as long as you know the secret, you can balance all day, no problem. Are you ready to hear the secret?"

"I'm ready, Daddy."

"Pedal. That's it. Just pedal. Isn't that an easy secret to remember?"

Caleb nodded sagely. "Got it."

Then we practiced almost exactly the same way as the day before. I was running behind the bike holding his seat, and he was pedaling. I pointed out that as he built his momentum, balance became easier. During this lesson, I'd occasionally let go of his seat and let him go for stretches on his own, running beside him all the while. I wanted him to focus on balance, and the key to balance was pedaling. Now, the first time he noticed that I'd let go, he squawked, "Daddy, hold on!" In that moment (and in the others when he began to doubt himself), I encouraged him: "You got it, buddy!"

Then I'd remind him of yesterday's outing: "What's lesson one?"

"No fear!"

"That's right! You own this!"

One time I let him go a distance without holding on to him, and he ran out of steam, slowed to a crawl, and fell over in the grass. He had a soft landing, and I scooped him up with encouragement. I literally picked him up with praise. He had lost momentum, which meant his pedaling needed a kick up in intensity. He had also successfully fallen and survived, so it was an opportunity to review both lessons.

I stabilized the ride by holding his bike seat approximately 75 percent of the time, and the rest of the time I simply ran next to him, building him up as he mastered both of the lessons we had covered. Each subsequent day, I stabilized him less.

After twenty minutes, he parked his bike with a smile and went in to report to his mom. I noticed he wanted to keep practicing, and perhaps that might have been a good thing. But my theory was that if he got exhausted, he'd start to regress, whine, complain, blame me for his failure to ride, and so on. His momentum was too precious to jeopardize. Instead, we parked after the appropriate time (with him intoxicated on the vapors of victory), and I figured he'd be excited for more. Which he was. For many of us, smaller lessons easily mastered are better than comprehensive lessons that overwhelm. And for Caleb, it worked like a charm.

Pedal Hard

This is a more complicated lesson than the first because it involves two concepts. How do you balance? You pedal. The only way to balance, as Einstein points out above, is to keep moving.

Imagine riding your bike downhill. You can balance easily while you coast, right? No effort required. You roll along with gravity, whistling a James Taylor tune, and pick up speed, all while the weight on the right side of your fulcrum of balance and the weight on the left side hum along in absolute symmetry. Gravity is your friend. So much so that you can almost remove your hands from the handlebars, place them behind your head, and take a quick nap.

When you bike uphill, how does balance look? Completely different. Inertia wants you down. Gravity hates your guts. It forces you to shift weight constantly back and forth as you pump hard with one leg, then the other. Not only do your legs pump to propel you forward, but your arms also pump the handlebars as you lean aggressively to one side, then to the other side. When you're climbing, balance is actually a dance of counterbalancing. But that's the only way to balance when you're climbing a hill, when you're working hard to propel your momentum upward.

And that's a beautifully accurate picture of how balance tends to look in life, family, work, and ministry most of the time. We rarely find ourselves coasting downhill. And as we seek the ride of our lives, we know that launching into a new adventure, whatever it is, will require an uphill slog.

As a happily married man and father of three who is also a pastor, I am joyfully and furiously attempting to balance family and ministry. Some weeks ministry and the satisfaction of accomplishment get the priority of the focus, and my family gets the short end of the stick. But when that happens, I try to lean heavily into family the following week. I rarely live a single week where the two are in perfect balance (coasting downhill). But in the dance of counterbalancing, I seek to consistently chart a course where both my family and my church know that they are cherished by me. It means that I have to be aware of how I've been leaning and intentionally lean in the opposite direction by saying no to certain commitments in order to say yes to balance. It also means I've got to be propelling myself forward, maintaining a crisp pace, because balance is impossible without momentum.

We have built three purposes into the core architecture of our church: love God, love people, serve the world. Jesus taught and modeled all three of these purposes, and so we staff, budget, and set ministry objectives along these lines. But it obviously begs to be balanced. It is a perpetual challenge to ensure that we are properly prioritizing all three of these purposes. We don't strike a perfect balance in any one moment (coasting downhill), but we do emphasize each one (we lean heavy into it), and then we shift our weight and lean into the next. We focus on, we highlight, we illustrate one (building momentum), then we ease off and shift our weight into the next. It requires a strategic calendar, planning our speaking schedule ahead of time, and looking closely at the projects we embrace and the ministries we fund. But without this dance of balancing and counterbalancing, we'd sacrifice the progress we've made in fulfilling our purposes.

Is balance a necessary part of your life? Of course it is. It's also a requirement if you're going to attempt a new, bigger, better thing. If you're going to learn the new skill or vault off into unknown territory, you've got to commit to it. But recognize that balance isn't something you can isolate and focus on without something else; you've got to create momentum. Make decisions. Move. Take action steps. As you move forward, you begin to balance. Balance has to be a priority, because if there is no balance in your life, you'll crash for certain. But balance can't be the only priority, because you have to move forward in order to accomplish it.

No matter what the area of focus is, you've got to be willing to pour in the effort required to generate forward momentum.

Balance Makes Us Stronger

My wife challenged me to join her in an Olympic-length triathlon this year (she has already completed a half Ironman), and I picked up the challenge (because it's hard on a guy when his wife is more of a stud than he is). A triathlon has three legs: swimming, biking, and running. I can do these three sporting exercises, but right away I realized that during the first leg I was going to drown. I'm a surfer (in exile). This means I only enjoy swimming with a large flotation device supporting me, called a surfboard. Without it, I'm plankton.

Even so, I soon understood that everything about triathlon training is designed to improve and increase your balance. From the repetitive swim drills (designed to help your equilibrium and perseverance in the water) to the biking drills (designed to help balance your muscle stamina and agility for any terrain) to the running drills (to improve steadfast balancing of pace regardless of course elevation change), each element focuses on balance.

But get this: training for all of these events together helps balance your body's muscle development, which helps prevent injury. Your body not only benefits by being more able to perform each one of these events individually, but the training for all three creates a unique balance of health and stamina that no single training provides. By way of contrast, a number of years ago my wife and I were training together for a marathon, and we logged hundreds of miles. But we both suffered injuries, me with an inflamed IT band, and Jodie with a stress fracture in her femur, by training so ruthlessly for this singular event. The training for the tri effectively strengthens all of the complementary muscles, which ends up preventing injury.

And this is how God has designed us to flourish when we are committed to creating the momentum required to balance. Think for a moment about your life and the roles that you want to fill with excellence. Visualize your core relationships flourishing. Imagine enjoying vocational achievement. See yourself nurturing intellectual acuity, embracing spiritual vitality, rocking physical health.

View them like training for the different events in a triathlon. By carefully giving momentum to each and alternating between them, you'll actually strengthen your performance in all. In no single week will you feel that you've achieved a perfect balance. But lean hard into the ones you can while propelling yourself uphill, and then next week lean into the others. Labor hard on some, and next month work diligently with others.

Pedal and Coast

> So with imagination, ingenuity and audacity, explore, discover, change the world. And have fun while you're at it. Always take time out to love and to live. You're going to be busy, but never forget family and friends.
>
> Daniel S. Goldin, administrator of NASA

It is true that some seasons of life require us to pedal harder than others. When riding a bike, some of the terrains we face require harder work than others. The same is true with some of the terrain we face in life. In some seasons, we're raising kids or caring for aging parents. We may face financial pressures that are difficult in this season and less difficult in the next, or marriages that struggle in some seasons and flourish in others. So be encouraged! No hill lasts forever. There is a downhill stretch coming. The seasons we face have a natural ebb and flow, so trust that God is with you and keep pedaling.

By the way, Jesus was a singularly great example of balance. Even while incredibly focused, he was not too busy to go out of his way to heal someone. He would minister to the masses and then retreat to the hilltops for prayer. He would hold rallies for thousands, and then he would withdraw to visit a town that had never heard of him. He would spend time building up the Twelve who were following him, and then he would enjoy some moments with just a few dear friends in relationships that were mutually filling. Jesus generated incredible momentum and lived a ministry, and life, in balance. We can too.

How do you balance? You pedal.

Now, today's youngsters are learning on bikes without pedals, tiny push vehicles called Strider balance bikes. I didn't know these sorts of things even existed when my kids were young. These push-bikes are so small that kids can start on them almost direct from the womb. But even with this tool, balance comes with movement. Even without pedals, balance can only happen in the context of momentum.

So get pedaling, thwart inertia, head-butt gravity, and go to work on balance.

Momentum

When a man asks himself what is meant by action he proves that he isn't a man of action. Action is a lack of balance. In order to act you must be somewhat insane. A reasonably sensible man is satisfied with thinking.

James A. Baldwin

When we began the lesson, I'd hold the bike for Caleb while he got on. I'd steady the bike and hold his seat while he got his feet in place and gripped the handlebars. And then I'd begin to walk with him, speeding into a jog as Caleb pedaled harder. It's safe to say that for the first couple of lessons, I was the initiator of my son's momentum. But we both knew the time was coming when he'd have to generate momentum on his own.

I met my wife for the first time at a Christian school event. I was the chapel speaker, and Jodie was in town from college, supporting her little sister who was receiving an award that day. Chapel had concluded, and Jodie's little sister introduced us. We had just begun a conversation when her parents, who were also there, invited me to breakfast with the three of them. So our first date was over pancakes with the folks. Jodie was horrified, certain her parents were attempting to settle a dowry amount before the third cup of coffee. After breakfast, I said good-bye and drove away. I could see all three of them in my rearview mirror, standing on the corner, chatting a bit more before Jodie headed back to the university. The sun was shining in a field of blue. The birds were singing. Jodie's yellow dress and long hair were rustling in the gentle breeze. And in that moment I thought, here was one I could give my heart to. I wanted to know this extraordinary woman more fully, and I wanted to be known by her.

Three days later, heart pounding, mouth dry, I gave her a phone call. I left a polite message, introducing myself again and wondering if she'd like to go on a date the next time she was in town. Maybe this time without her folks.

That was nineteen years and a million miles ago. I'm so very thankful she said yes.

Now Jodie and I have the daily joy of balancing life and work and family. But that's only after momentum begins. Action is required before balance. Without the initial phone message (which was saved and played dozens of times for the amusement of many, apparently), there would have been no additional dates and the relationship would never have flourished. Initiating movement is the prerequisite to balance.

Without movement, you can balance for a second. With it, you can balance forever.

All Activity Does Not Equal Productivity

Organizing the paper clip drawer doesn't help anybody.

Carefully choosing the actions we take is essential when it comes to embracing momentum as the key component to bringing balance into our lives. We must choose to tie our time and energy to things that are close to the priorities of our love and faith.

Once, when Jodie and I were newly married, we had good friends who were coming over for dinner. Our little apartment was a total mess (this was pre-children), so we decided to invest the seventeen minutes it would take to completely clean it. This was a good thing, because our friends were arriving in roughly fourteen minutes. Instead of picking up the laundry from our living room couch or carrying the dirty dishes from our table to the sink, I rather absently took down the cappuccino machine from the top of our refrigerator and started polishing the dust off of it. Jodie looked at me like I had espresso for brains. "How about start with the dishes? How about push the vacuum? There are some really big needs right in front of us, you hot hunk of a husband"—I think I'm remembering this correctly—"so let's start there, and then if that gets taken care of, then we can focus on the minutia." She was right. I think this is an important reality to embrace, no matter what scenario we're in. Momentum is best generated when we push first on our priorities.

Do the Right Something

If you're Noah on the ark crammed full of animals, and the boat starts to list to one side, you move the elephants, not the hummingbird cage. The challenge with building momentum is not simply to *do something*. The challenge is to *do the right something*.

At some point, you have to realize that if you're perpetually living life out of balance, that is your choice. In the final analysis, you are responsible for determining your own priorities. You can blame it on your job, your finances, your upbringing, or your relationships for only so long.

My buddy was working in sales for the world's most profitable company at the time, in downtown Chicago. One day he was driving his toddler son and his wife by his office, and from the car seat in the back, he heard his son exclaim, "Daddy's house!" And my friend realized that his son believed he lived with Mommy in Mommy's house, and that his dad lived in another house: the downtown office.

After this revelation he began some hard conversations with his wife first, and with his boss second. But ultimately my friend ended up leaving that company and finding another way to provide for his family. He wanted his son to know that his parents actually lived together in the same house. He had no desire to look his son in the eyes after twenty-five years and tell him that Dad missed his childhood because he simply chose to be gone. So he made a move. It was the momentum he needed to help him get his life in balance.

Momentum Begins with Beginning

My wife and I have lived in our current house for nine years. Every year we've dreamed about remodeling our downstairs living room. We've dreamed about ripping out the carpet, staining the concrete floor, and replacing our fireplace with a more efficient gas-burning insert. But we never seemed to have the time or space in our budget to do it.

I should mention that I'm about as handy as a three-year-old with a plastic tool set. But this is something that needs doing. So a couple of days ago, my wife and I just jumped. We moved everything out of the room, and I began to tear out the carpet. I used a hammer to remove all the tack strips. Jodie talked with the guys at Home Depot about renting the concrete buffing tool we'll need, and she selected the stain color for the floor. As I was removing the carpet, we realized that we'll also need to demolish the tile floor in the bathroom, and why not redo that one at the same time? And of course the old fireplace needs to be removed to make room for the new insert.

The beginning of a project usually reveals other new projects to begin. As I write this, the whole downstairs looks like a war zone. We're pedaling as hard as we can up the steepest, most uncomfortable sort of hill there is in our world. And yet I know that now that we've begun, the project will move to completion. As you are reading these words, the remodel is either completed (I'm writing this in faith) or we've decided to just leave it and move. If we would never have begun, the work would never get done. But now that we've begun, the momentum we've generated will guarantee that the project will happen.

Imagine pushing down on a pedal, hard, to begin your forward motion. Once you're moving, less force is required, but the first pedal needs great force. Picture the initial amount of fuel and fire required to launch a rocket from the pad upward into the heavens. The majority of thrust is used in the first few seconds as the rocket builds momentum. Get a mental image of the locomotive starting to chug forward and the amount of energy and time required for the engine to begin to move all of the cars forward the first few feet. Once momentum is achieved, maintaining it takes far less effort. But initiating momentum is monumental. Momentum begins with beginning. The first step is always the hardest and the most important.

Jim Collins, in his book *Good to Great*, talks about a flywheel. A flywheel is like the crank of a bike. It takes an incredible amount of energy to push the flywheel, especially from a state of rest. Bodies at rest tend to stay resting. But an amazing thing happens as we keep pushing the flywheel forward: it begins to lend its own momentum to our efforts in pushing it. And at some imperceptible instant, the effort that we have to exert is minimized because the flywheel has built up energy on its own.

Due to gravity and inertia, it will now propel itself forward as long as we continue using a minimal amount of our own effort.

I've seen this happen again and again in life. I've seen it happen in marriage. I've seen it happen in ministry. And I've seen it happen as balance is prioritized. The momentum we will generate by pedaling helps move us into a dynamic state of balance.

Because our spiritual lives so often get neglected, I recommend generating momentum in yours. The most incredible moments of my life are moments of intimacy with Jesus. The greatest days I have are days of enjoying my relationship with God. I don't always live there, often because the demands of life in a chaotic, fast-paced world beckon me to lean into other tasks. But as soon as I can, I lean back into Jesus, giving him time and space to speak to my heart. I find that moments spent with him are always a great investment, propelling me forward, providing a productive momentum that helps me to better live the balance I desire. Remember, God loves you and is holding you. He will help propel you down the best pathways of life.

You Can't *Think* Your Way to Balance

You can't *think* your way to balance. You have to move toward it. Even if God is the one instructing you, directing your steps, you're the one who is responsible for moving. That's why we keep cycling back to momentum.

We must choose to pedal toward balance-producing momentum. Each of us must be willing to push hard to take the ride of our lives. The Bible tells us that *with faith all things are possible*, but we are never told that all things are easy. Just the opposite. In fact, with most good things in life, most new adventures, most dreams fulfilled, significant effort is required. We must never be afraid to work hard to see great things accomplished through our lives. And even though there isn't a single area of life that doesn't require balance, we won't ever see it if we don't commit to generating momentum in our lives.

So live with a green light.

Unless the Lord himself closes a door, assume it's open. The apostle Paul did. One time God closed a door and wouldn't allow Paul to go where Paul thought he wanted to go. One time. The rest of the time, Paul lived as a man of action.

Initiate momentum.

Move.

Pedal.

7

Balancing Act

Man maintains his balance, poise, and sense of security only
as he is moving forward.

Maxwell Maltz

When you're riding a bike, the only thing you have to balance
is the left side of your body against the right side. Even as I
was running around the yard with Caleb, holding his bike seat
and talking about balance, I realized how pervasive this lesson
is in life. Balance is required virtually everywhere.

I heard about a study that was done on how people communicate with hand gestures. Generally, people who use an
appropriate amount of hand motions while they are speaking
are viewed as warm, open, and friendly. I'm a communicator,
so this is good news for me. But then I learned that too much
gesturing communicates that the speaker is frantic and insecure.
And too little hand movement indicates that the speaker is
cold, distant, and unfeeling. Then there are some hand gestures
that are never positive, such as pointing at the person you're

speaking to, because it communicates domination over the listener. The more informed I became about hand gestures in communication, the more stressed I became.

This reveals how much nuance is required in just a simple concept like utilizing hand gestures in communication. Too many and you're viewed as Chicken Little; too few and you're the Godfather. Point once with your index finger, and suddenly you're the vice principal in charge of discipline. What is required? A balancing act.

Entire sports industries are built on this foundation of balance through momentum. Snowboarding. Surfing. Skating. Wakeboarding. Once you move and build momentum, balancing successfully is an act of fine-tuning and constant adjustment. It's a dance of counterbalancing. Nuances must be managed. If balance isn't considered, you could think you're sailing when you're already in the process of crashing.

Nobody can strike a perfect balance every time, in every area. But there are several situations in every life where an honest heart endeavors to thrive. These are essential areas of life where the dance of counterbalancing needs to be appropriately prioritized and prayed over. Below are the crucial tensions worthy of negotiating a balancing act.

Work/Life

I was talking to a friend of mine named Kelly, and the topic rather morbidly shifted to what we wanted carved into our tombstones after our life journeys were complete. Kelly said what he wanted engraved on his was the words, "He Wished He Spent More Time at the Office." I laughed out loud, because Kelly is a big family man who loves his wife and children extravagantly. When I asked him why, he answered with a grin, "Just going against the flow."

There are no easy answers when it comes to the work/life balance. There are hundreds of books on this topic alone, and here is the CliffsNotes version of helpful advice: make this balancing act a priority. Schedule in family time because what gets calendared gets done. Be willing to reevaluate how important career pursuits are in terms of how you want to live. Be willing to downsize material desires to upsize relational quantity and quality. Be willing to say no to good things in order to say yes to great things.

Speaking/Listening

In relationships, asking questions is a far more positive and powerful tool than speaking wisdom. What we say is less important than how we ask and how well we hear. So often in the middle of a conversation we realize that we are merely waiting for our turn to speak. No wonder many of our relationships are shallow. Much of the friendship is just an inner dialogue with ourselves. If you find yourself finishing another's sentences, institute a pause before you take your turn speaking. Ask yourself, "How would a truly caring person listen?" And then listen like that. Focus on asking more questions and making fewer statements. Seek to be fully present so that you can hear the other person's heart, not just the words.

Fun/Discipline

With children, I am constantly tempted to be the fun guy. I have to fight this tendency and engage in the harder tasks of discipline, of coaching in the difficult moments, and of conflict resolution between siblings. Most parents, I'm guessing, fall naturally on one side of this tension or the other, which means that they must generate momentum by pushing hard on the other side. If you're finding yourself always being the heavy, practice lightening up and having some fun with your family. Remember to enjoy the dance of counterbalancing.

Structure/Flexibility

Some people live highly structured lives, while others live with spur-of-the-moment spontaneity. Whichever side you naturally fall on, embrace it, and then lean heavily on the other side at times. If you constantly "drop everything and go," then challenge yourself to plan the details well ahead of time for a family event or a special date with your loved one. If you honestly can't get spontaneous, then program in your "spontaneous" ideas ahead of time, and just don't tell anyone. Everyone else will think you're being spontaneous, and you'll still be in your wheelhouse.

Spending/Saving

Our church teaches about finances through Dave Ramsey's Financial Peace University, and we have got several pastors on our team who are big fans of Dave. My wife and I are walking the simple road of Dave's Seven Baby Steps.[1] We view his materials as helpful for stewardship of God's resources. However, the one change we make as we present clear financial coaching is this: generosity must be balanced into any plan we make. It's not something to be set aside until there are no other financial burdens. Giving is designed by the Lord to simply be something that we figure into our weekly stewardship.

Health/Living

Health has obvious benefits. Each one of us mere mortals is a unique blend of body, mind, and spirit, of chemical reactions and eternal being. So it's important to seek to be emotionally, intellectually, spiritually, and physically healthy. We value purposeful work. At the same time, it is important to value sleep, recreation, and laughter. And yet, when fun becomes the only value, health declines. So living and fun must be balanced with health and discipline. The truth is, you could work out, eat right, sleep well, cut down on salt and alcohol, avoid smoking, eat only bland protein and flavorless vegetables, and still get hit by a bus. So be healthy, but also live a little.

Selfishness/Self-Care

Don't be selfish. We cover this truth quite often in church, in school, and at home. But since we've heard it so much, many people (moms especially) neglect to care for themselves at all. Too much self-care is selfish, and your key relationships and career will suffer in the shadow of your self-focus. However, to deny yourself care and to not value yourself at all can create an internal bitterness, a martyr syndrome, and all relationships suffer under this tyrant as well. Remember, a complete lack of self-care is ironically a form of selfishness.

Depth/Shallowness

In our relationships, every one of us has friendships that are meaningful, as well as many acquaintances in which we are friendly but not close friends. This happens to be my weakest balancing act of all. I am completely at home in fun, polite, and relatively shallow relationships. Swimming there, I'm like a fish in caffeinated water.

Once, on a vacation, I took my family boating off the coast of Hawaii. We got into a pod of spinner dolphins. The guide instructed us to applaud, and when we began to clap and cheer, the dolphins began to jump and spin in joyful earnest. That's how I naturally feel in five-minute friendships, like a spinner dolphin leaping to applause—which is fine, and I can lean into that since part of my job is to love and connect with thousands. However, I know I also have to do what I'm not comfortable doing and push hard to take some of those relationships to a deeper level.

Action/Patience

Action versus patience describes the tension between doing it myself versus waiting on the Lord in faith.

I believe the Lord loves to come through big-time for us. He loves to wow us, to knock our socks off, to blow our minds. I also believe that he invites us into the work with him, to allow us to live lives of impact and significance, so that we experience the joy of being a part of what God is up to in the world. It seems to me that as we move in faith, God meets us and yields a phenomenal return on our investment.

My buddy Dan works with a ministry called Special Delivery that provides housing and care for women in the midst of crisis pregnancies. It's a home that also offers help to young moms who have already given birth, and many stories of love, wholeness, and victory have come from this ministry. Dan had a dream of opening a little thrift store to peddle secondhand baby supplies on a dumpy little corner within easy walking distance of the ministry. Then Dan heard about a friend who was looking for property to build a $21 million dollar Alzheimer's care facility in our area. So Dan pitched him the dumpy little corner. If the deal goes through, not only will the property value be increased, but additional homes could be opened up for Special Delivery. And the new building would include a storefront for the baby supply thrift store. Plus, the new development would open up potential jobs, easily accessed, for our young moms to serve and care for Alzheimer's patients. We are currently praying in faith for this development to go through.

This is an example of waiting on the Lord, even as we seek to balance serving him by acting with diligence. And it's an example of the exponential power of God and his delight in blowing away our expectations.

Don't Balance This

The only thing I don't recommend balancing is love. Be unbalanced here. Just love. Again and again. As much as you can. Outlandishly, even.

You don't need to be especially skilled, educated, or connected to love outlandishly. An eight-year-old boy named Ethan heard that it cost $1.92 to provide a meal for a homeless person at our local shelter, and he had a desire to help a few hungry folks get fed. So he decided to give his allowance to buy a few meals. Then he thought he would empty his savings to buy some meals. With both his savings and his allowance, he was able to purchase around fifteen meals.

Then Ethan challenged his parents to join him and do the same. So they put together a donation page, challenged all of their Facebook friends, and talked about it with their church family, which happened to be my church family. I might have mentioned it from the pulpit. Then the local news got wind of Ethan's challenge. At last count, Ethan has provided over eight thousand meals. Jesus fed five thousand with loaves and fish, and then he said we'd do even greater things. Here's an eight-year-old feeding thousands more with nickels and dimes because Ethan leaned into love without worrying about balance at all.

Live Unbalanced

At the evening of our life we will be judged on love.

Saint John of the Cross

I believe we must live balanced in almost all things, except love. The Lord loves unconditionally, he loves unfailingly, he loves limitlessly. I believe God is unbalanced in his love, and I want to be like that.

So in the way I interact with Caleb, even if he is frustrated while he's learning to ride and lashes out at me, I want to make sure I'm a steadfast communicator of love, no matter what.

In fact, in the way I engage with all my family and friends, I want to love them wildly, hugely, in an over-the-top sort of way. But recently I've felt Jesus challenging me to live unbalanced in love for everyone I might come across, not just the ones who are easy.

As a pastor, I get a lot of love, a lot of hugs and high fives, and a ton of affirmation. But pastors also take shots. They get the negatives, criticisms, and complaints. Occasionally people don't like what we do or don't like how we do it, don't like the fact that I'm hobbit-sized or that I look like Spicolli from *Fast Times at Ridgemont High*, don't resonate with the self-deprecating humor that I use, and so on.

So every year, we do this thing called Easter. It's a big deal in the church world. We invite the community, and our folks bring their friends. We're prayerful, purposeful, and intentional about literally everything we do, because we know that on Easter Sunday we get to share with people we haven't seen in a while or might not see again in a while. We don't do anything on Easter that we don't do the other fifty-one Sundays a year, but we're just aware that it's open house for us; it's like Super Bowl Sunday, and so we use just a bit more spit and polish. I don't think any of this is different for our church than it is for yours.

Last year Easter was fantastic. We celebrated thousands and thousands in attendance and hundreds of spiritual decisions for the Lord. We invited seventy-five of our folks to share the reason they trust Jesus on what is called a "cardboard testimony," and we received almost a thousand positive responses. These were people who were moved, folks who brought friends and followed up with them, people who found joy serving. That weekend was exhausting but so rewarding; God was definitely on the move. So the week after Easter, when I got a letter in the mail, I opened it, thinking, "Fun! Another letter from a heart set on fire." But that's not exactly what it was.

It started off, "Dear Pastor Mike," which sounded pleasant enough. It continued, "I'm writing to express my concern about my experience at church last Sunday." Suddenly my mood shifted. I tried to get my mind around what was so concerning. I was going to show you the whole letter, but it depressed my publisher. Instead, I'll paraphrase most of it, and I'll try to be generous as I do.

It started with, "I have never been so disappointed about a church service on a special Sunday like this ever before." Turns out, she uses the word *disappointed* quite a bit in this letter.

She mentioned that she used to attend Overlake but changed to another church a few years ago. She had been back to Overlake a few times to hear me speak, but she had been disappointed each visit. For some reason, she said, she ended up at OCC again for Easter, but she pointed out that it was a mistake she wouldn't make again. She was disappointed in the music, and even though the room was filled with people, she was disappointed that they weren't worshiping God in the sort of way that she expected. She might have mentioned that she "endured" the service.

She also said, "I was disappointed with your sermon." That quote was followed by her assertion that I failed to engage her heart as well as challenge her mind. She mentioned that she felt sad and empty from the experience. It sort of mirrored my feelings as I read her letter.

After two more paragraphs detailing her disappointment (bringing the total number of times she used the word to eight), she concluded, "I wouldn't recommend Overlake. I doubt that I will return again. Sincerely and in Him"—and she signed her name.

I want to give you some insight into my processing, and it's not all pretty. This letter landed like an uppercut on my spiritual jawbone, and not only did I feel myself reeling but I had a bunch of other responses. I knew the author of this letter and knew of her decision to trust Jesus with her life decades ago. I knew her pattern of serving and giving and knew of her decision to attend another church. So this wasn't an anonymous person tossing a hand grenade; it was criticism from a legitimate source and merited a response from me. The only problem was that I was truly wounded by her perspective and the way she chose to communicate it.

Drafting a Response

So I began to compose letters to her in my mind. (Do you ever have conversations in your mind? You know you do. I've seen you talking to nobody in your car.) Because I took it so personally, the first letter I crafted in my mind—I'm being frank with you—was not the right way to go. In fact, you'll see it was the wrong way to go. The first letter was a short one that started and ended with the words, "Get behind me, Satan. Sincerely, and in him." And I meant it sincerely. Those words of disappointment are Satan's words. He's the one who whispers all the time, "You aren't good enough. You're ridiculous. You're shallow. You're not compelling. You're disappointing."

If you want to get pastors to quit, simply tell them they suck. They're the ones hanging themselves out to dry every single week. They're the ones living in a glass bubble, stressing to make sure that all parts of their lives are a legible billboard pointing to Jesus, so just tell them they might as well not bother. Tell them you're disappointed seven or eight times in a single letter, and make it be the only time they've ever heard from you. Satan is the one who seeks to discourage, to depress, to dishearten. So the next time you're tempted to go to a pastor, any pastor, and unload on him or her, just think about this: it's not God who is fueling that fire. It's God's enemy who wants that pastor, and every pastor, discouraged. And chances are your pastor is doing a good enough job at discouraging himself or herself and doesn't really need your help.

If your heart is to help, then help. Pour courage in. Serve alongside. I'm serious. Church work is bizarre and confusing, and on the front lines the sniper bullets are everywhere, like a scene from *Apocalypse Now* where it's difficult to tell the difference between the Fourth of July and Armageddon. Your pastor needs your help, not your critique.

That's the letter I wrote in my mind. I didn't send it.

In the second mental letter I crafted, I went through the transcript of my message for Easter. I pulled out every truth and the theological and biblical reasoning that went into my points, which were intentionally designed to be simple: Why did the cross have to happen? Why was the resurrection a necessity? Why Jesus at all?

Through the simplicity of this structure, I was able to unpack the whole gospel, and hundreds of people personally embraced a saving faith in Jesus. So I thought about asking the author of this letter, "Exactly what parts of God loving the world so much that he sent Jesus to be crucified and resurrected for the sins of humanity, and the invitation to step into eternal life with him, did you find particularly shallow and unmoving?" I didn't send this one either.

The third letter I wrote mentally—and this is just anger talking—went something like this: "If it was my goal to put together a service that aimed to please the entitled Christian Pharisee, to entertain the frozen chosen, and to play the songs that would make the already convinced feel all warm and fuzzy, then you're right, I was *way* off. And by the way, where was the nonbeliever you were bringing with you on the most evangelistic Sunday of the year? And why didn't you partner with your home church on Easter? I know that church and I know that they too were wanting you to bring a nonbeliever with you because they don't want to create an environment where the home crowd simply shows up to critique the entertainment value of their service any more than we do."

I'm not sharing these thoughts because I think they're the right thoughts. I'm only sharing them as a sort of insight into my journey, the pain I was feeling, and my struggle to craft a legitimate response to signed criticism. I didn't send this letter either.

In the fourth letter I wrote in my mind (and yes, I had better things to do with my time), I thought about sharing one anecdote from the Sunday service she had attended. "Let me tell you the story of my buddy, a dad on a soccer team that I've coached for the past five years. Let me tell you how I've watched him go through this evolution in his life. A couple years ago his wife left him and the kids after she'd had a number of affairs. Of course he's crushed, reeling, trying to figure things out. He begins dating a gal he really cares about, and they end up getting pregnant. That wasn't the timetable that anyone was hoping for, but they both want to make the right decisions with the circumstances they are facing. So they chose to stay together and have the baby, and through this season they've begun coming to Overlake Christian Church (OCC) as a family. I know that he's still trying to land on where he stands with life and faith and marriage. But on Easter Sunday, they were all there, the entire clan sitting in the front row. I could tell he was tracking with the message, an active listener. Sometimes as a communicator you can tell when someone's with you, and I could tell he was with me. And when the cardboard testimonies started, when dozens of people began to share what they are trusting Jesus with in their lives, he began to weep. Tears began flowing down his face. He was shaking. His shoulders were heaving. He was so emotional that he pulled his shirt up over his eyes, and his girlfriend was sitting there stroking his back, whispering her love to him, telling him it's okay, it's okay. God was doing something miraculous that day. God was renovating a heart that day."

I felt like saying to the woman who wrote the letter that the Easter services I went to were filled with God's Spirit moving, and showing grace, and loving, and inviting, and I was sorry the Christian show wasn't up to her standards, that the spiritual entertainment didn't meet her expectations. But Jesus is *alive* and transforming hearts. (By the way, I followed up with my buddy, and God did in fact rock his world that day, and last August I had the honor of ministering at their wedding and getting a front-row seat to see God's redemption and healing in a broken and hurting world.)

But even though that was a true and honest response, I knew inherently that it wasn't the right response. None of these responses felt right, even though I felt justified in thinking them. I just didn't feel that any of them led to freedom. Jesus models and teaches us to be outlandishly loving, to be unbalanced in love, and I want to walk in his footsteps. He's the one who prayed, "Father forgive them," over the very ones nailing him to a cross. I started thinking, "I don't want to win the argument; I want to win the heart." I remembered the old truth that a bulldog can beat up a skunk, but is it worth the stink?

What would Jesus call me to do if he were crafting the response? I decided to send the writer of the letter a bouquet of flowers. My administrative assistant and I mailed her the spring bouquet arrangement from our local florist. I wrote a short note, the only message I actually crafted and sent, and it said simply:

Got your letter. Praying good things this year, for both of us. Blessings.

Pastor Mike

As I wrote it, I sincerely prayed life and blessings over her. And I experienced the pleasure of the Lord. What I felt was Jesus meeting me in that decision, going, "Yeah, that's it. Take it higher. Take the conversation higher. Lift your eyes higher. Love like I love you—outlandishly." Was sending a bouquet of flowers in any way a proportional response to her letter to me? No. It was outlandish.

Another Letter

I wasn't expecting any further correspondence, and maybe didn't even want an email back, because I wanted to just release it to Jesus, release her to Jesus, and get on with my life. I had some things I actually needed to do. But I did get an email back, and I'm thankful.

She said the flowers had arrived that day, and she thanked me for the totally unexpected gesture. (Really? She didn't see that one coming? Shocker.) Then she said, "Yes, we need to pray for good things this year. You have no idea how timely that message is for me. Thank you."

You don't know what other people are going through. You don't know what roads other folks are walking. You don't know the pain in others' lives, which is why I don't think you will ever regret walking the road of intentional, radical love. I know it's a harder and higher road to walk, and sometimes it's a heart-wrenching road to walk. But the right road to walk is the road of outlandish love. It's a "turn the other cheek" road, a "lay down your life" road, a "bless your enemies" road, a Jesus road, but it's the right road.

I want you to understand that God was not disappointed with our services on Easter. He was glorified. Neither was he disappointed by our response to the criticism of our services on Easter. He was glorified again. And he will be glorified in you and me as long as we love outlandishly.

I want to start a movement of loving folks outlandishly, creatively, winsomely—where the whimsy and beauty of Jesus leak all over as people just get loved radically. Again and again. In a completely unbalanced way. This is *not* the way to ride a bike. But it is the way to follow in the footsteps of Jesus. The recipients of love are people who may be desperate for love and people who perhaps aren't deserving of it. It doesn't matter. Just love. Love. Love. I want outlandish, creative love to be a part of my DNA. I know I can't love everybody extravagantly. But if I consistently build love into my priority list, then when

God shows me the opportunity, I'm ready to engage, ready to lavish, ready to pour it on.

God is the source of all love, so we gain momentum to love by going to him. There is nothing balanced about the way he loves us. His love is everlasting. His love is unconditional. His love is unfailing. And I want to love like that.

Caleb needed to focus on balance in order to successfully ride his bike, and the key to his balance was momentum. He needed to pedal. You and I have to focus on balance to live well, to embrace the new adventure God is inviting us into. There are going to be many things to keep in mind, to hold in dynamic tension, to embrace in the dance of counterbalancing. But one thing you don't have to worry about balancing is love. In this one regard, we are free to live unbalanced.

Lesson Three

Steering

Steering

Go where your best prayers take you.

Frederick Buechner

On day three Caleb had a ton of energy. There was just something special about day three, with blue skies above, birds singing in the sunshine, and victory on the horizon. Caleb had chatted to my wife about these lessons he was mastering. She was simultaneously thrilled and perturbed that Dad got to show up as the guru of cycling after she had previously invested many frustrating sessions with our son. (Let it go, babe. Let it go.)

"Caleb," I called, "it's time to tackle another lesson." He scrambled to grab his bike and met me out in the driveway with helmet on. I held his seat as he got on. He began to pedal.

"So, Caleb," I said, "this is lesson three: steering. Steering is how we avoid obstacles."

He repeated this to me with the uniform consistency of a soldier's marching song. "Right, Dad. Steering is how we avoid obstacles."

Yet even as he voiced this, he was looking at the ground, watching himself pedal and heading for the side of my car, so I actually had to lift his chin. "Bud," I said, "you've got to look up. You have to look ahead to avoid obstacles, but there's an even better reason to look ahead." I said, "You have to keep your head up, because where you look is where you'll go." I let him pedal for greater and greater stretches without my hand to balance him. And like our lessons previously, we talked the entire time.

We launched into review. I asked him, "What's lesson one?" and he said with a smile, "No fear!"

"Why no fear?"

"Because my dad's got me!"

"That's right," I said. "I do have you. Now, what's lesson two?"

"Balance!" he joyfully yelled.

"And how do you balance?"

"Pedal!" (There was a lot of shouting.)

"Excellent. Now what's lesson three?"

"Steering."

"Right. It is what we're working on now. And why do you have to keep your head up?"

"Because where you look is where you'll go."

It's true. In life as well as in biking, you'll go where you're looking. Your direction determines your destination. Where you focus, you'll gravitate.

As I was pondering this lesson along Caleb's journey, it made me ask a very foundational question: Where do I want my life to go? In what direction do I deeply desire the journey to head? What destination am I stirred to pursue? And I realized what I want more than anything. I want to steer my life into a magnificent story.

Elvish, Anyone?

Speaking of stories, I'm a Tolkien nut. I confess this while being aware that I live in Microsoft country (aka geek central) where the fourth most-spoken language is Elvish, and a commonly concealed weapon on this side of Seattle is a dagger named Sting. I've got maps, framed artwork, and Aragorn's sword hanging on my office wall. I've read everything J. R. R. Tolkien has written, including all of the stuff normal people have never heard of (*Unfinished Tales? Leaf by Niggle*, anyone?). I am head over heels for Middle-earth, mostly because early in high school I got turned on to *The Lord of the Rings* and would come home from football practice, grab my book, and enter into a mystical land. It was as if I'd strapped on a sword with some glorious heritage and journeyed along with dwarves, elves, and hobbits led by Gandalf the wizard. In my imagination, I would join in their misadventures, which I found to be exciting, moving, and humorous. I was such an avid reader that if my parents wanted to punish me, they couldn't send me to my room, because that's where I wanted to be anyway, reading Tolkien. They punished me by banishing me from my room. "You get out here and enjoy your family, young man!" I'm a sucker for a good story.

There is a practical reason why most of the Scriptures are narratives, why they are told in story mode. The culture and history of the ancient Israelites were transmitted by storytelling. Around tribal fires, over many generations, narrative truths were passed from one to the next, and these truths were more easily remembered and understood handed down in the form of story. God is interested in telling an amazing story. We respond to God's story because we're made in the image of the storyteller.

We Are Hardwired for Story

We all love good stories. We love to hear them, we love to tell them, we love to watch them unfold. It's hardwired into us. Now, we've lost a bit of this along the information super-highway. With today's barrage of status updates, tweets, bullet points, and a twenty-four-hour news cycle, it's a "just the facts" world we soldier through. Stories grab us, move us, inform us, and provide us with a setting in which to understand our universe. In fact, I'd argue that the most powerful thing in the world, the thing the world is longing for most intently, is a good, heart-stirring story. Think about how good stories breathe life into your soul. Notice the way these beginnings whisk us away:

> "Once upon a time . . ."
> "A long time ago, in a galaxy far, far away . . ."
> "In a hole in the ground there lived a hobbit . . ."

But the greatest story ever told starts with the words, "In the beginning God created the heavens and the earth" (Gen. 1:1).

What Happens Next?

And so begins the great true story of God creating and loving and redeeming. In fact, not only does God create, love, and redeem, but God invades. The Bible contains story after story of how God covers the natural with the supernatural, how he reveals the miraculous, how he dispenses hope, how he shows up in power to open a way where there is no way, how he provides, and how he invites mere mortals to join him in the adventure of bringing his kingdom here to earth.

As a daddy, I've logged hundreds of hours reading to my kiddos, sitting on the couch with my son Caleb reading Hardy

Boys stories or snuggling my boy Duzi in his bed reading *The Hobbit* (just in time for the movies to come out). And every single chapter we read brings up all sorts of questions: Why did he do that? What's going to happen next? How are they going to get out of this one? Do they live happily ever after?

This Is Your Life

In Deuteronomy we are told to start with telling our children and our family members the incredible story of how God's love has invaded our world. That's a great place to start. But it doesn't end there. Think concentric circles of influence. Think ripples flowing outward from your splash in the pond of life. This is why we must steer our lives into great stories. We touch others with the impact of our story.

In fact, I hate to break it to you, but you're already telling a story with your life. With how you manage your days. With how you invest your time. With how you engage relationships. With how you interact with those in your world. It's either a story filled with life and laughter and hope or it's a story filled with fear and sorrow. And you never know how intently, how diligently, nor how often your audience is listening, because the most powerful thing in the world, the thing the world is longing for most intently, is a cracking good story. So steer yourself into one.

How Does It End?

Last year I threw my jaw out of joint at the Melting Pot. Are you familiar with the Melting Pot? It has nothing to do with the recent marijuana legislation in Washington. The Melting Pot is where you pay a ton of money to cook your own food. They bring you raw meat and veggies, and you cook it in their fondue cookers and then dip it in all of their delicious sauces, and the final course is chocolate, so when you're done you roll out of there with an empty wallet and tumble right into a diabetic coma. It's a good deal.

The waitress walked us through all the sauces, which ones tasted good with the bread, which ones tasted good with the veggies, which ones to use with the steak, the chicken, the shrimp. She said something about how the angry sauce tastes best with the lobster, but be careful because it's a bit spicy. It didn't look spicy; it innocently looked like cocktail sauce. So when I cooked my bit of lobster, I dunked it liberally into the angry sauce and popped it steaming into my mouth. The waitress said it was a bit spicy. What she didn't tell me was that the angry sauce was one part cocktail sauce, five parts horseradish, and three parts rocket fuel. Angry was an understatement. That sauce was furious. It hit my tongue and howled up my nose, and I jerked my head to the side so hard that I threw my jaw out of whack. The angry sauce just snickered.

That's not the interesting part.

The interesting part is that several months later, I was visiting my sister in California and we were hanging out with our kids in a public pool. I was telling my sister that story, and suddenly we both glanced up from the pool where we were talking, and there were six people listening intently. One lady said, "Well, go on. How does it end?" I finished the story feeling a little self-conscious. Especially since I was wearing a Speedo. (Just kidding. It was a thong.)

My point is that you never know who is listening to your story. You never know who is watching your life.

There has always been an open invitation for God's people to share the story of how God's love is invading this fallen world through our own stories.

What Story Are You Steering Into?

My buddy Joseph told me last year that his dad shared with his family the full story of God's invasion into his life. He wrote about his early journey through Buddhism and into Hinduism and how his road finally led him to a place of deep depression. One night he was so tired of living that he went to a high-rise hotel and attempted to jump out the window. At the last moment, he felt an invisible hand pushing him back into the room. He assumed God wasn't willing to let him find an end. It frightened him, but he didn't try again. A few days later, someone handed him a Gideon Bible, and he flipped to the back where there was a sample prayer to pray, and he prayed, gave his life to the Lord, and has followed him ever since. Not only was that a story Joseph had never heard, but it became a huge blessing of God's love to Joseph and his family.

When I was a youth pastor, we'd do these high school community gatherings where we'd ask students to share about their faith journeys. When the whole group was gathered, we'd say, "Hey, let's hear from some of you. How is God working in your life? Anyone can feel free to grab the microphone and share." Our more confident students would typically share first, and this would usually prime the pump for other kids.

On one night, the energy seemed to be especially high as students began to share how God was invading their lives, how he was showing up for them, how he was blessing and providing for them. Just a few student leaders shared first, but then a few more did, and a few more, and soon I was running all around the room with the microphone, feeling amazed at the freedom the students felt during this time.

Finally, after about two dozen students had shared, a girl I didn't recognize asked for the microphone. It was her first time at youth group. She said, "I am not a follower of God. I don't know anything about Jesus. I just came tonight with my friend Jackie. But after hearing the stories of how God is working in your lives, I decided I want to give my life to him." We prayed with her right there and led her to trust the Lord amid the tears and laughter and great joy of her peers.

You never know what kind of impact your story will have.

Can I Get a Witness?

> But you will receive power when the Holy Spirit comes upon you. And you will be my witnesses, telling people about me everywhere—in Jerusalem, throughout Judea, in Samaria, and to the ends of the earth.
>
> Acts 1:8

The word *witness* has never particularly resonated with me because it reminds me of a legal term used in a court case (and I'm not particularly excited by the law). I prefer to use the story motif. "You will be my storytellers. . . ." That I can do, and so can you.

Steer your life toward a better story. Ask God to tell a story through you, to turn your life in such a direction that adventure and joy and healing and wholeness and purpose are all a part of your story—the story of coming alive in an ever-deepening and dynamic relationship with the Father who loves you.

The world is dying for a good story.

> Come to me with your ears wide open.
> Listen, and you will find life. (Isa. 55:3)

10

Turning in God's Direction

I used to think the future was solid or fixed, something you inherited like an old building that you move into when the previous generation moves out or gets chased out. But it's not. The future is not fixed; it's fluid. You can build your own building, or hut or condo. . . . The world is more malleable than you think and it's waiting for you to hammer it into shape.

Bono, humanitarian, musician on God's iPod

While riding, Caleb was looking at his feet, at the ground, and even at the crank as it went around and around. As he was doing that, he almost hit my car, the mailbox, our dog, and a little towheaded kid named Liam whose hair looked like a feathery dandelion gone to seed. In riding, as well as in life, you need to look where you're going.

For most of us, that means keeping our heads up and boldly facing the future.

In order to get anywhere, you have to look at where you're going. How do you envision your investment in college paying off? How do you want your business to operate? How can you maximize your ministry at church? How do you want to glorify God in your job, neighborhood, classroom, community? How would you desire your friendships to flourish? Ultimately, wherever your focus is, that's where you end up going. Where you look is where you'll go.

If you listen to the promptings of Jesus when you look ahead at your life, then together you create a vision of where you'd like to go. Ask him to give you the next steps to get there.

Steering into an Adoption Story

Jodie and I felt that God was nudging us toward adoption, and five years into that journey we are so thankful that he did. Duzi, our South African son, is a constant source of joy with his quick smile and open heart. He has been an absolute blessing, but every adoption comes with unique challenges. For example, his full name was Mduduzi Shozi, which is a beautiful Zulu name. We wanted to keep his first name, and we were pretty sure he'd be the only Mduduzi in his class. But we wanted to give him a middle name that was more familiar to American ears, in case he wanted to switch things up at some point in his life.

That's a unique problem, because what name sounds good following Mduduzi? You can't just go with Mduduzi Bob. Jodie and I wrestled and prayed, and we landed on Ezekiel. Mduduzi Ezekiel Howerton. Mduduzi means "comforter" and Ezekiel means "God is his strength." Duzi carries both comfort and strength, and we are so thankful for the gift of parenting him.

Zulu Launch Party

I want to recount one experience from our adventure of bringing Duzi home from South Africa. When we pulled up to the house where he was staying, he was waiting at the gate for us, all shy and quiet and excited. The house mom, Liz, asked him, "Do you know why these folks are here?" And in a precious accent that has long since faded, he said gently, "They've come to fetch me."

Duzi had lived in a children's home in Durban from the time he was about eighteen months old until we picked him up at age five and a half (or as he told us, "I am five and a million"). He was well cared for by Liz and the other staff. And there were a number of youth workers who knew and loved Duzi as well. So after spending over a week with them and finalizing the court process with all the paperwork, we were ready to collect Duzi's things and begin the long journey home. But all of the women, men, and youth workers who had invested in his life wanted to gather around and send him off well. Jodie and I didn't know what to expect. Actually, there would have been no way for our American minds to anticipate what they had in mind.

From what I can gather, the Zulu culture is quite expressive, communicating emotion through song and dance. So when we brought Duzi around to say good-bye for the last time, twenty or so folks had gathered, each one of whom had invested some of their heart into the life of my son. They began to sing and dance over him. Their tribute was spontaneous but beautiful, choreographed yet unrehearsed. They expressed themselves with incredible rhythmic and vocal repetition.

We asked, because the singing was in Zulu, and were told that the songs they were singing over him were songs of blessing, songs of grace, and songs of love. They were singing guidance over him and celebrating his new life, his new family, and the new adventure he was about to embark on. There were smiles and tears and at times uproarious laughter.

Finally, we gave all our hugs, loaded up his things, and began to drive away, waving and honking. And as we drove down the street, we realized that the youth volunteers were running as fast as they could after our car, hooting and hollering. We were literally propelled forward with their whoops of joy. We were carried forward on the songs of their well-wishes. To this day that moment remains one of the most beautiful of my life. I will forever be indebted to their love and celebration and belief in the future of my Duzi. (When I wrote this paragraph I cried. Jodie had tears on her cheeks as she read it. We are just so humbly thankful for the outlandish love our family has received.)

Jodie and I had looked ahead in the direction of God's prompting and begun to walk the road of adoption. The house mom and youth workers in Duzi's life had looked ahead to envision *his* future and give him the best launch into his new life that they knew how to give. And now that we are together as a family, the challenge remains for us to look ahead so that we can live healthy, grow strong, and experience the adventure God has for all of us.

When I talk about looking ahead, I'm really talking about being aware of your goals—acknowledging and unpacking the desires God has placed deep inside you, understanding the dreams stirring within you, and then steering your life in their direction.

What's Your Dream?

We all have dreams. According to the king of dreams, Walt Disney, a dream is a wish your heart makes. Our dreams can range from big to little, from grand to humble. Some of us have dreams to be the president, play in the Super Bowl, win the lottery, visit a tropical island.

Some dreams seem much different, like dreaming of getting through a day without fighting with a spouse, dreaming of not wondering where the next dollar is coming from, dreaming about having a satisfying relationship.

Others are kingdom-shaped dreams of bringing the love of God to a village in Africa or leading your own family to embrace the grace Jesus offers.

Regardless of the tenor of our dreams, we are all dreamers, each and every one of us.

God's Multicolored Kingdom

Martin Luther King Jr. is a big deal in our house (since we're an interracial family living in King County), and we are grateful for his contribution to the civil rights movement. Our family benefits daily from his dream. It's interesting to note that he is best known for his "I Have a Dream" speech, not his "I Have a Strategic Plan" or his "I Have Formed an Exploratory Committee" speech.

His dream was to live in a nation where boys and girls with brown skin and boys and girls with peach skin (these are the terms that Duzi operates with) would play together on the hill and have equal access to education and prosperity. While we still have a distance to go in our nation, the truth of the matter is that I'm profoundly thankful for this dream and for all those who dreamed this same dream, because every night I tuck my kids in bed and see a picture of a little piece of that dream coming true.

Of course, King's dream remains powerful because it didn't just benefit him. It benefits all of us. He did not just dream up some man-made construct or something that would glorify an ego, but he envisioned a part of God's kingdom becoming a reality within our fallen kingdoms. He dreamed of what a bit of heaven could look like on earth and painted the picture of how different our nation would be if people were to see the image of God reflected in each other.

Fire in Your Bones

At our church, we set up a thirty-foot-long chalkboard in the hallway, and I invited our congregation to dream and to share their dreams with the rest of their church family by writing them in chalk. I invited everyone to participate. I wanted to give everyone permission to dream and freedom to be aware of their dreams. It turns out that dreaming is intergenerational, universal, and biblical.

A dream encapsulates your heart's desires. It identifies your deep yearnings, your passionate imagination that lingers. If you're wondering, "How do I know this is a dream?" the answer is that it will burn like fire in your bones. Not just a passing fancy but *fire*. And this is where you need to steer your life; this is where you need to be looking as you pedal and balance.

A dream is like a glorious haunting. You put it out of your mind, and it just keeps coming back, again and again and again. Submerging a dream is like trying to hold a beach ball underwater. You can do it, but only for a while, and then it bobs to the surface again. This is what God is calling you to. This is the "bike" he's inviting you to learn to ride.

God Knows the Dreams He Has Planted within Us

Several years ago, I remember hearing a man speak on pursuing our dreams, and afterward I had a conversation with a mom who had two small children. I asked her, "What did you think of that message?" She replied, "To be honest, I'm so exhausted and so busy, with so much of my time owned by others right now, that I don't feel like I can dream." She needed space and permission.

I want to give you permission to dream. God desires to shape your dream and guide you as you pursue your dream, but right now I want you to breathe deeply and simply know that it's okay to dream.

Can our dreams get delayed, sidetracked, broken? Of course. Jeremiah 29:11 says, "'For I know the plans I have for you,' says the LORD. 'They are plans for good and not for disaster, to give you a future and a hope.'" Even as this passage in Jeremiah was being written, the Israelites were being carted off to Babylon, their dreams dashed against the rocks. In that moment, God wanted them to know, "I've got you. I know your dreams, and I want to meet you there."

God is a Father who loves to bless his children. Part of our problem as humans is that we don't trust that God wants to bless us, or we aren't aware that he *is* blessing us. So we take things into our own hands. And often, this is when we wind up on detours filled with potholes, broken pavement, and dead ends.

In Us and through Us

Some dreams are about what God wants to do *through* us. Other dreams are about what God wants to do *in* us. As my buddy Scott says, "God doesn't use us to get projects done. God uses projects to get us done."

My dear friend Pastor Gilbert was walking through his town when he felt that God was stirring his heart for one of the impoverished corners of his city. His city is Delhi, India. He continued to walk and to pray, and God birthed a dream in his heart that Gilbert would plant a church in a slum. Gilbert planted. Then he began to walk through another slum, and God was stirring his heart for that place to have a church as well. Through prayer and planning, Gilbert began to plant churches in these areas.

Finally, he decided to get strategic, and he grabbed a map of his city and drew a grid over it. He began to pray that God would allow him to plant a church in each coordinate on the grid. God met him and guided him, and he began to see his dream being fulfilled. After a while, Gilbert felt God leading again, so he did the same thing with a map of his state. And once more, his dream became reality. Now Gilbert has drawn a grid over the nation of India, soon to be the most populated country on the planet. His dream is that he will be able to plant a church in every grid coordinate on the map. Along the way, hundreds of thousands of people are coming to know the love and grace of Jesus. But none of it would have happened if Gilbert hadn't looked ahead at where he dreamed his life would go.

Ask for whatever you want God to give you. Delight yourself in him, and he will give you the desires of your heart.

When it comes to steering ahead into life and adventure, you need to understand that God puts dreams within us to work like a compass. They are our own personal North Star, intended by God to help us navigate. I want to encourage you to look ahead at where your dreams are calling you to go.

He Does This All the Time

Once, when I was just out of college, during a surf trek with my buddy Barry from Puerto Escondido to Jaco, Costa Rica, I found myself on a rickety, overcrowded bus. It was an overnight trip to our next destination, and around 2:00 a.m. the bus headlights went out. The bus slowed abruptly, which was what caused me to rouse and see what was going on. What I saw was the bus driver sticking his hand out the window to shine a flickering flashlight on the ground ahead, increasing speed, and continuing to joyfully careen along the coastal cliffside roads of Mexico in the dead of night. I was petrified for half a moment, but I reckoned, "He probably does this all the time," and went back to sleep.

As you begin to steer your life in the direction of the dream God has planted in your heart, you won't be able to see all the way to completion. This is where faith comes in. You won't be able to see the whole road. But God will show you, like a flashlight pointed at the ground ahead, how to steer along the road that you need to take. Trust him. He does this all the time.

The Way You Look Matters

Nothing contributes so much to tranquilize the mind as a steady purpose—a point on which the soul may fix its intellectual eye.

Mary Shelley

When I was in college, I spent some time overseas in Pepperdine's study abroad programs, once in Heidelberg, Germany, and once in London, England. I spent quite a bit of time hitchhiking, which means I spent a little time hitching and a lot of time hiking, backpacking all over Europe, with friends and on solo treks.

One day I was alone, traveling through the thick, rainy Welsh fog. I was hiking over the crest of a hill and saw a gray refinery or something. It had lights on it yet looked like a factory that had been vacated. But it was far off in the distance and difficult to see clearly through the cloud, so I was unsure. But I kept traveling toward it. Through the mist, I'd crest a hill and think maybe it wasn't a factory, and then I'd dip down and not be able to see it for a bit, and then I'd crest up over a hill and it'd become a bit clearer, and I'd think maybe it was an abandoned waste management plant. The closer and closer I got to it, the more my perspective would shift. I was almost sure that it was a refinery, then I was certain it wasn't, and suddenly I realized that it was, in fact, a castle. I laughed out loud. I had been thinking like an American, and castles are rarely on the horizon this side of the pond.

Your perspective determines greatly what you see. The way you look will determine where you turn the handlebars. What I thought was maybe a waste management plant was actually the heart of an ancient kingdom where once dwelt an ancient king.

Look Alive

Looking down can be painful and depressing. Looking behind can be dangerous, as even the most novice biker knows. Both could leave you in the ditch.

The challenge is to look clearly and joyfully ahead. How you turn your wheel matters. What is the story you want your life to tell? What are the dreams you have for your life? What do you hope to accomplish? Who do you want to be? What kind of character do you dream of having?

My buddy Mark calls it utilizing your sanctified imagination. One way to employ this is to imagine who you will be in heaven. What kind of person are you going to be when you stand before Jesus, perfected? What will your desires be, what will your hang-ups be, what will your habits be when you're standing in the presence of God? Imagine that future you, and then set your course for that destination.

By the way, the Lord delights in assisting you in becoming this person. He loves pouring truly good gifts out into your life. In the first chapter of James, we read that every good gift comes from God our Father. During his ministry, Jesus said that God, in all his grace, showers blessings on both the righteous and the unrighteous. And he challenges those who will listen that if we really want to be the children of our heavenly Father, we'll do the same. Jesus came to paint that kind of picture of God's undeserved favor. That's the story he steered his life into.

The King and His Castle

For example, in the ninth chapter of Matthew, in one short passage starting in verse 18, Jesus heals a bleeding woman, raises a little girl from the dead, gives two blind men sight, and casts a demon out of a man, returning the use of his voice. That's a full day for Jesus, good time management. He's pedaling hard.

But the whole thing looks like a broken-down factory. It looks like a waste management plant in disrepair that smells even worse. Yet in the midst of the mess, Jesus brings the kingdom and uncovers the good heart of the king. Jesus was revealing beauty where it had been hidden. He was revealing life where everyone else saw death. Jesus was ending isolation. He was piercing the darkness. Jesus was making the broken whole. And in each one of these instances, Jesus saw clearly ahead and displayed the heart of our eternally good Father. Jesus didn't pretend there was a kingdom. He revealed it.

When Jesus began his earthly ministry, he did it by reading this scroll from an ancient biblical prophecy in what we now call Isaiah 61:

> The Spirit of the Lord is on me,
>   because he has anointed me
>   to proclaim good news to the poor.
> He has sent me to proclaim freedom for the prisoners
>   and recovery of sight for the blind,

to set the oppressed free,
> to proclaim the year of the Lord's favor. (Luke
> 4:18–19 NIV)

And when he finished reading it, Jesus announced that this prophecy was now fulfilled. He declared that these verses were about him, and among other things he proclaimed that the time of the Lord's favor is now.

Princess Creates Prince

Many years ago, my wife and I were in Florida for my brother's wedding amidst a humid swelterfest in July, and the day after the reception when all the other family members were heading to the airport to return to habitable climates, Jodie and I decided to take a day to explore the Magic Kingdom. It was hot enough to melt lead, so what sounded really fun was actually standing in line for hours sweating profusely next to other people sweating profusely.

One difference between the Disney parks is the castles. In Florida, it's Cinderella's castle (not Sleeping Beauty's) and they have an elegant restaurant inside, and the restaurant has air-conditioning. That was the draw—the entire draw. Jodie and I were so excited about the AC that they could have been serving cat food and we'd have been fine.

We made reservations, and we arrived twenty minutes ahead of time to cool off in their castle waiting room. The room was rather crowded with families all waiting to be taken into the castle to enjoy a meal. We noticed a family of three standing nearby. It was comprised of adults, a man and his wife, and a second gentleman in a wheelchair who had a beard, the two men looking as if they were brothers. But the man in the wheelchair was unable to force his muscles to obey him. His back was arched, his fingers and arms were askew, his mouth was open in a contorted leer, and there was spittle on his beard. I remember thinking how uncomfortable he must be in the suffocating heat.

As we were waiting, Cinderella came in to greet her guests. With all the dignity, beauty, and refined mannerisms of a princess, she came to each group waiting and welcomed them warmly. She didn't spend much time with Jodie and me, as we were in our midtwenties with no kids. She waved at us, and we were like, "Hey Cindy." But then she made it to the man in the wheelchair. She greeted him, and he began to shake back and forth with excitement. He was obviously pleased, grinning, his arms waving a bit, and he tried to say hi to her, but he could only moan a bit, and more spittle landed on his beard. She gently shook his hand hello, and then she just held it for a moment while they spoke.

"Hello. Welcome to my castle. What's your name?"

The man standing next to the wheelchair answered, something like, "This is Grant."

"Well, Grant," she said to the man in the chair, looking straight into his eyes, "you have a beautiful smile. Thank you for sharing it with me. I hope you enjoy your lunch very much." As she floated away, the whole room got shimmery, and I had this huge lump in my throat, and in the happiest place on earth my wife and I found ourselves in tears.

What was so beautiful was the way she was able to redeem and redefine the situation. "You have a beautiful smile." She didn't lie and pretend that what was in fact ugly was somehow beautiful. Her presence and grace literally wrought a transformation. With her holding his hand, looking into his eyes, his smile *was* beautiful. He was beaming and bright and joyful, and because she was a princess, he suddenly, for an instant, had become her prince. Disney calls itself a Magic Kingdom, and she had chosen to share that magic in an instant where it was needed. When she held his hand, she didn't lose any beauty at all; instead, they both were made more beautiful.

That's what Jesus did. Again and again and again. In the eighth chapter of Matthew we read about a man with leprosy who knelt before Jesus and cried out, "Lord . . . if you are willing, you can heal me and make me clean" (v. 2). In an astounding move of paradigm-shifting proportions, the Bible says that Jesus reached out and touched him. Jesus held his hand. Jesus gave him a hug. "I am willing. . . . Be healed!" (v. 3). Touching the leper didn't make Jesus unclean; instead, it made the leper clean. It's as if for a moment the whole thing looked like a broken-down factory, but Jesus showed it was actually a castle, and the King's heart is really good.

Represent!

> We're Christ's representatives. God uses us to persuade men and women to drop their differences and enter into God's work of making things right between them. We're speaking for Christ himself now: Become friends with God; he's already a friend with you. How? you say. In Christ. God put the wrong on him who never did anything wrong, so we could be put right with God.
>
> 2 Corinthians 5:20–21 Message

Jesus is God in the flesh, representing God's heart and revealing God's favor for his people, and the story continues in our lives. We are the representatives. We re-present Jesus. That's our job. That's our road map. That's where we need to steer this thing.

When I was hitchhiking, I found a refinery that wasn't a refinery and a waste management plant that wasn't a waste management plant but was actually a castle at the heart of an ancient kingdom and the seat of a noble king. How I looked mattered.

This is the way it works. When you look at yourself, what do you see? All of your faults and insecurities and shortcomings? Or do you see a son or daughter of the King?

When you look at this world, when you interact with the people in it, you're not experiencing it; you're defining it. Is it a broken-down factory? Or is it a castle with a king ruling over his kingdom? What Jesus never did was pretend, "Oh look, if you squint and tilt your head just right, you can almost imagine this chaos and mess looks like a kingdom." What Jesus always did—like with the leper, like with the woman caught in the act of adultery—again and again, and what he continues to do today is act, move, love, display beauty, and show if you will let him that God can use your willingness to reveal his kingdom right where you are.

If you'll let him, God can use your life to write his living story. But only you get to choose how to steer. Where you focus, that's where you'll go.

The way you look matters.

12

Avoiding Obstacles

If you do not change direction, you may end up where you are heading.

Lao Tzu

Right now, the car I drive is a 1999 Saturn wagon that smells inside like little kid vomit, moldering goldfish crackers, and wet dog. (This is not a step up from the Mustang I drove in high school. More like a fall from grace.) It has many, many, many miles on it, and when I drive I have to keep one foot on the brake and one on the gas, or else it will die in all kinds of embarrassing places. It smokes and revs and occasionally refuses to start, mostly when my friends happen to be standing around, eliciting their pity-smiles. Truly, this car is poetry on wheels. Bad poetry. A dirty limerick. Every time I get where I'm trying to go, I count it an example of God's common grace over my life.

But the best perk about driving this beauty is that the windshield wipers glitched out a year ago. Think about that for a moment. No windshield wipers. In Seattle. Living here is like living in the produce section of the grocery store, under the lettuce misters. There are only nineteen days a year when windshield wipers aren't required. That leaves 346 days a year when I've learned how to make it work. I know the secret: if you look *at* the raindrops on the window, you'll crash and die in a fiery heap. If you look *through* the raindrops, you'll get where you're going every time.

Obstacles are like raindrops. Focus on them and they'll get you off course every time.

Look through them, keeping your eyes fixed intently on the road ahead, and you can safely get where you're going.

> The LORD is good and does what is right;
>> he shows the proper path to those who go astray.
>
> (Ps. 25:8)

What does this mean, the proper path? It means God helps us steer. It means we can allow God to guide our lives. It means that even when we hit obstacles, the Lord leads us through with grace. Jesus prompts us along the path of victory.

As you're steering toward your best life, you need to be aware of the obstacles that will predictably and unexpectedly pop up in your path. When that happens, you will need to not give up on your dreams but offer your dreams to God so that he can sculpt them according to his wisdom and grace. You may need to course correct. You will certainly need to change direction if you discover you've lost your way.

Getting Lost

Once I went hiking with a few of my buddies to the top of Mount Adams in southern Washington, a twelve-thousand-foot peak. It took us around six hours to climb to the top, first to the false summit, then to the true summit. When I got to the top, I was dazzled, light-headed from the exertion, dizzy from the beauty of being on top of a glacier, on top of a mountain, on top of the world.

What took us hours to climb up along the ice trail with crampons and ice picks took us forty minutes to come down glissading. Or as we call it in my family, *butt-surfing*. This is when you lean back on your keister and shush down the glacial slope like discarded members of the Jamaican bobsled team. But as we vaulted our way down fields of ice, whooping and hollering and having this out-of-mind type joy ("I'm sliding down a mountain!") we lost the trail.

When we reached the bottom of the glacier, still quite a distance above the timberline, we simply could not find the trail we had ascended on. We spent hours tramping around, trying to find it, feeling that somehow we were hiking around the circumference of the mountain in the wrong direction. It began to get dark. We were just below the glacier, just above the timberline, without food, out of water, sans sleeping bags. My buddy Ron said that we would freeze to death unless we got naked, spooned together, and piled our clothes on top to protect us from the cold. I told him I'd had a good life. We were just beginning the conversation about which one of us had the most meat on his bones, in case survival required cannibalism, when we heard the guy who drove us to the trailhead call our names.

We went crazy with joy. "We're over here! We're over here!"

He said, "Why did you guys stop? Why didn't you come on down the trail?"

"We were lost! We had no idea where the trail was."

He turned and pointed not fifty yards from us. "It's right there." As in, right here. We had camped almost on the thing. It was literally at our feet.

No matter how lost you think you are, the path from death to life starts literally at your feet. Jesus is always near to show the proper path to those who go astray.

Good Obstacles

Sometimes obstacles can be pleasant, an overabundance of blessing. As ironic as it seems, one obstacle that takes people out is early success. In order to steer properly toward the goals that God is giving us, we'll need to trim some good things out. (In Proverbs 10:22 we learn that the Lord brings the increase and he adds no sorrow with it.) The overabundance of good things can be a bad thing when it prevents us from pursuing the one thing that God wants for us.

Sometimes obstacles are hurtful things, like relationships that have a negative impact in your life or habits that pull your integrity down, limit your effectiveness, or prevent you from living the story that God is prompting you to live. Obstacles can be anything that prevents your bike from functioning well. And there will always be circumstances you must endeavor to change so that you can pursue your vision (for example, lack of training, debt bondage, and not having a supportive community).

Only you can steer your life. So craft the space to dream, be aware of your dream, and share the dream stirring within you. Dreaming is important, has power, and can make a positive impact on the world, mostly because it is the single greatest tool for steering your life.

God Can Redeem Broken Dreams

God can work through even the most broken of dreams, even the most tragic circumstances, and draw good out, resurrect joy, open up new windows of hope, reveal new vistas of adventure. He can also make original dreams come true in a fun and unexpected way. God is not put off by the obstacles we face.

Proverbs tells us that the fulfillment of dreams gives life. This is because the permission to dream is given by God himself. We are invited to delight ourselves in the Lord, and then he will give us the desires of our heart. We are invited, like David was invited, to ask for the nations. We are invited, like Solomon was invited, to ask for whatever we want. We are invited, because Jesus invites us, to ask our Father for anything in Jesus's name. (See Proverbs 13:12; Psalm 37:4; 1 Kings 3:5; Psalm 2:8; and John 14:13–14.)

God receives glory when he fulfills the dreams that he's planted within us. This tree of life we enjoy when a dream is fulfilled brings God our Father such glory. But we also must recognize that many dreams are broken and feel broken.

God Can Choose to Interrupt Some Dreams

We say, "If this happens, I will take it as a sign from God." "If this door opens, I'll take it as a sign he wants me to walk through it." "If this opportunity fails, I'll take it as a sign God wants me to stay put." This is like Gideon laying a fleece out before the Lord (see Judges 6), and I believe there are many times the Lord meets us at the fleece.

God is involved in our dreams, and he's not afraid to disrupt some of them. He will not give us the blessing that will destroy us. That's the kind of merciful Father he is.

For example, if my son Duzi were to ask me for a chain saw, I'd say "not yet." As an eight-year-old, he's not ready for it. I don't trust his muscles, and I don't trust his motives. "Buddy, there is a better tool for opening the jam jar," I'd say. "You know what? Let's get another tool for trimming the dog's toenails."

But there will be a day, someday in the future, when a chain saw would be an appropriate blessing, especially if he lives in some kind of zombie apocalypse, or in Yakima. Same thing.

Sometimes God graciously allows us to achieve our dreams, only to help us realize that they weren't really what we wanted. Once, when my son Caleb was three, our family was on vacation. We had wandered into a store in the resort town we were visiting, and Jodie told him to pick out whatever he wanted from the store as a special treat. Instantly he became incredibly focused and began to hunt through every aisle, evaluating, calculating. He picked one item up and carried it around for a while. Then he put it down, but he wandered back to it again. He asked me if he should get this item, and I told him that would be fine if it was what he really wanted. He pondered and weighed his choice for some time. Finally, he brought his item to Jodie and said, "Mommy, this is what I want." "Really, buddy?" "Yup." She purchased it for him, and he carried it lovingly out of the store. He had picked out a spatula.

Honestly, I'm not sure how much joy that gift brought him. We still have it. It's great for eggs. But sometimes it happens that we get our kids what they want, even when we know it isn't the thing that will bring them deep joy. God will occasionally do the same for us.

Some Obstacles Are Caused by Our Choices

We can default on some dreams by the choices we make. God actually allows us to see ahead. Some of us are gifted to see farther ahead than others, but all of us can see that our actions pay the dividends of consequences. While we might not be able to see all of the obstacles we'll face, we can see many of them.

My buddy Aaron wanted to work for the CIA (names have been changed to protect the shady), so there were some things he opted out of along the course of his young life. He passed on some activities and some parties. In college we'd all be heading out, but not Aaron, because he had this dream of working in the CIA and knew that if he wasn't careful, he'd default on that dream—because they were probably watching him. And they're probably watching you. Sorry. Pretend not to notice.

We do have the ability to default. Think about a job a young man can't get because of some choices he made that ended up on his record. Think about relational choices that aren't healthy and lock us into a path that forces us to abandon a dream. Or think about how pride in a relationship can end up pushing people away from each other. You can imagine financial choices we make in a moment that take years to recover from. You can imagine moral choices that build a burden and carry consequences that must be shouldered. There are all sorts of scenarios we could paint of people who have defaulted on dreams.

I'm convinced that one of the primary reasons God hates sin is because he sees that sin can be such a dream thief. He loves us and stirs dreams within us, and he sees how our sin (and others') steals those dreams away. And he hates it.

Obstacles Can Be Difficult Circumstances

Devastating things happen in this fallen world. Tragic occurrences rock us and rip our dreams to shreds. There may be no answer. There may be no quick relief. If you or a friend of yours has lost a child, you know that the unnatural progression of a parent outliving a son or a daughter rocks the universe. There are some pains that are fully eased only by the balm of eternity. This is the meantime, and it can be brutally mean.

I'm thinking of Ellen and Chet who buried their five-year-old, Jackie. I'm thinking of Rob and Linda, who buried their twenty-year-old son, Ryan. Of two friends who have buried their infant son, or two other friends who asked me to conduct the funeral of their elementary-school-aged son. I'm also thinking of people facing scenarios that are incredibly difficult and unlikely to change. Blake and Mackenzie thought their daughter had a heavy dose of sensory processing disorder, but it turned out to be a syndrome even more rare and difficult. Her functionality seems to be getting worse as she grows; her behavioral outbursts are getting more violent and difficult to manage, and this is a heartbreak of another sort. Another difficulty is when an adoption hope ends because despite months of careful work and prayerful connection a birth mom changes her mind. Mostly we celebrate that as a good thing, but it's also sad for willing parents who go home to an empty house with a nursery and a crib all set up for a baby, and there's no baby, and those are dreams crushed; those are hearts broken.

Most of what I can offer, most of what you can offer, is just your tears acknowledging that the intrusion of this kind of grotesque pain in this broken world hurts so very much. Ninety percent of helping is just showing up. But even then, you can humbly offer Jesus, the one who said, "Blessed are those who mourn, for they will be comforted" (Matt. 5:4 NIV). He is our wounded healer. He is our source of comfort. He will meet us and walk with us. Even then, you can humbly remind those in pain that this wound does not get the final say, and that one day all tears will be wiped away.

In the midst of a fallen world, we cling to the Lord and steer our lives on the path he shows us. When circumstantial obstacles conspire to crush our dreams, we cling all the more steadfastly to our Father's direction. We take the broken pieces of our shattered dreams, and we offer them up to our Dad. We trust that he has us, even now. We trust that he will hold us and steer us forward. And we, through tears and heaving chests, ask him to take our broken dreams and redeem them. We ask for our dreams to be restored by his loving hand.

Dreaming a New Dream

> The best time to plant an oak tree was twenty years ago. The second best time is now.
>
> ancient proverb

In the pale thin afternoon sun of a winter day, I was half dozing at my computer and half thinking about the kinds of dreams we dream.

Our dreams are fostered by our hopes. They're shaped by our limitations. They're encouraged by our lovers and friends. They're discouraged by those who fear change. And the thing is—the greatest thing of all is—that the One who thought up dreams in the first place is so often found somewhere within them.

In the dreams about addictions being broken and relationships being fostered or mended, we see the evidence of the Lord of wholeness and the Lord of love.

In the dreams about adopting children, or combating human trafficking, or working to be an agent of cure for the HIV pandemic, we see evidences of the King making his kingdom known right in the middle of this broken-down factory.

In the dreams about sharing Jesus with a friend or a loved one or with millions, we see the evidences of a Savior who is so winsome and unpredictable that he doesn't want anyone to be left out of the fun. In the dreams of going to a specific region, to employ a specific task, in order to alleviate a specific problem, we see the Lord of details, who is not only vast enough to reconcile the whole universe to himself, but intricate enough to love the individual, to meet the need.

And since I was nearing a dream myself, I dreamed that all of our dreams would be swallowed up in one great kingdom-sized dream, that all of our dreams would come to fulfillment, bringing the reality of the kingdom and the glory of the King like never before.

It was a dream of hope.

Then the sun faded, and the coffee kicked in, and I found myself in the cold, wet, February winter again. But I choose the dream, and the wonderfully mysterious God this dreaming represents. I choose to walk in the hope that his dreams bring. And I encourage you to dream God's dreams, to look through your obstacles, and to steer your life in the direction of his hope as well.

Braking

How to Slow and When to Stop

Now and then it's good to pause in our pursuit of happiness and just be happy.

Guillaume Apollinaire

By the time lesson four rolled around, Caleb was feeling his oats. He was radiating confidence as he met me in the driveway, standing ten feet tall, grinning like a Cheshire cat. I held his seat for him as he started off, and then I let go as he zealously pedaled, balanced, and flitted around our yard like a meandering butterfly. He kept his head up and didn't look at the ground, or me, and was able to successfully steer through our yard, over our driveway, and around the shrubs. Of course we reviewed each of these lessons verbally.

"What's lesson one, pal?"

"No fear 'cause my dad has me!"

"What's lesson two?"

"Balance with pedaling!"

"And lesson three?"

"Steering!"

"How do you steer?"

"You look where you go and you go where you look!"

I was excited with him. He was well on his way to vehicular mastery. So I said, "Buddy, you're ready for lesson four. It's braking."

He shouted out, "Watch, Dad! I already know how to stop!" So I watched. I watched him slam on the brakes, stop abruptly, and fall over. As I helped him back up on his bike, I placed my hand on his feet and showed him how to gently apply the brakes by pushing consistently against his pedals.

I tried to help him get his mind around braking. I told him, "Buddy, braking is pushing steadily against the way you were just pushing." He repeated this carefully. "The problem with slamming on the brakes is that it upsets your balance, though sometimes it's necessary to do, like in order to avoid a parked car or mailbox or telephone pole that darts out in front of your path. But most of the time, you're going to want to use your brakes to *slow down*." Caleb was already good at locking his leg muscles against the pedals, so the real work was in helping him press against the pedals in a measured fashion.

We practiced that discipline as we worked on the previous lessons, again for twenty minutes, and then celebrated with high fives and lemonade.

When you push against your pedals, or squeeze the hand brakes on your bike, you are exerting a force that slows your motion. When you first begin to ride, all of your energy is focused on creating momentum, on accelerating. Slowing requires friction. Braking is the first lesson that seems to come against what we've been building thus far. "Pedal to balance! Steer fearlessly! Wait, now pedal backward!" It seems counterintuitive, but it is essential to be in control of the friction we employ to slow things down.

The challenge is to be able to brake in life as well.

Push against the Way You Were Pedaling

There are times when we need to push in the exact opposite direction from what we've been pedaling so hard toward. This sounds insane, but half of mastering a thing is learning how to go, and half is learning how to stop going. Think about downhill skiing. Have you ever seen a beginner on the slopes take out an entire ski lift line? Plowing into body parts and getting concussions as your go-to braking method is a sure sign you're not yet ready for the black diamond runs.

When it comes to the new adventure, the new skill, the new direction you're going to explore, you need to understand that you're going to have to use the brakes on some of the things you've worked hard to get in motion. Why would you want to do this? Because in order to create the space in your life to say yes to the new adventure, to steer toward the kingdom dream, you must say no to the old. You simply cannot continue to add more and more and more momentum to your life without slowing and stopping some of the things you've been doing.

So when it comes to pushing against the way you were pedaling, the first step is to push back into your love of God. Ask him to make it clear what you need to take a break from. And he will answer you. Leaning into intimacy with the Lord will bring both clarity and joy.

By Necessity, Braking Employs Friction

Friction has the ability to hurt a bit. Friction always causes a little heat. Driving north from Southern California on Interstate

5, you hit a stretch called "the grapevine." As you descend several thousand feet of elevation in a short stretch of road, there is a perpetual smell of brakes being ground down to nubs. Friction just burns them up. It's always fun to be driving down in front of a fully loaded eighteen-wheeler, imagining friction turning his brake pads to vapor.

If you choose to apply the brakes anywhere in your world, there will be friction. People will not understand. They will say things like, "But I thought you wanted to do this thing." "You were really doing well in this. Why would you want to give it up?" "You have worked so hard to make this happen. I don't get why you're choosing to walk away."

I don't know what the friction will look like for you or where it will heat up your world. It might manifest itself as friction with the status quo of your work culture. It might be friction with the normal accepted breakneck speed of family activities. Friction might cause pain in friendships as you evaluate where you spend your time.

This is why the previous lessons are helpful—live fearlessly, pursue balance, steer well—because as a son or daughter of your heavenly Father, you have clarity about the life that you are called to live. This perspective allows you to graciously and gently walk through the inevitable friction caused by applying the brakes.

Slamming on the Brakes Causes a Lack of Balance

Caleb experienced the problem of slamming on his brakes on his bike, and you'll experience this in your life. It doesn't mean you should never do it; it simply means that in order to do it, you're going to have to prepare to stop. On a two-wheeler, you're going to have to be ready to put your foot down so that you don't fall over. What do you need to do to be ready to slam on the brakes?

After twenty-one years in ministry, I was granted a study break by the elders at my church. I was out of the pulpit for three months, and for two of those months, I was leading ministry trips and working on a writing project. But for one month, I just got to be dad and husband.

Now, this break took a bit of preparation. I had to plan ahead in order to maximize the space, prepare for my departure by scheduling others to teach in my absence, and ensure that the ministry direction and culture would continue unabated (I have the honor of working with senior associate pastors who are phenomenal). I also had to prepare myself and schedule time with other pastors, schedule time at other churches, and schedule a plan to be personally productive so that I'd feel victorious. I had to prepare my family for the new schedule.

All of this did cause a bit of friction, but it was well worth the preparation. As a family, we ended up making a list of fifty activities we were going to enjoy over the summer, and we were able to accomplish forty-two of them. I was so thankful for the extravagant gift the elders gave me. The Father used it to breathe new life into me, to give me his abundant joy. I am still so humbled and grateful for the gift of time. When I stopped going forward at a sprinter's pace, braked, and rested, God refilled my energy, replenished my creativity, and restored my passion.

I want to encourage you, as a son or daughter of our heavenly Father: practice slowing. Stop what you need to stop. And don't be afraid of the friction it will cause, but instead be prepared for how God wants to meet you through it.

What Doesn't Matter, Doesn't Matter

Last Thursday I spent the afternoon with my friend Tamara who is dying of stage four metastatic breast cancer. There is quite a bit of pain associated with her condition, and she's just been diagnosed with congestive heart failure. This is big-time. Final stretch time. She has some friends who have adopted her, who have sort of formed Team Tamara, and they've been bringing her meals, taking her to the hospital, and giving her two girls rides when needed. She calls them her love village. My wife is crazy about Tamara, who is wry, brilliant, and irreverent. When I can, I take my turn bringing firewood to her home so she can enjoy a fire, or picking up a prescription for her, or taking her to the hospital for her to get IVs and scans and pain meds. I'm like an alternate on Team Tamara.

Today I stopped by her hospital room in Seattle, which had a view of Puget Sound and the mountains between the city and the sea. Tamara is forty-six years old without a single wrinkle (which amazes me, because my leather face is well crossed with laugh lines and furrows, like some kind of tiny, crazy farmer has been plowing drunk on my face while I'm sleeping) but with a wicked dry sense of humor. She told me that at her funeral she doesn't want any spiritual clichés. She doesn't want any of God's greatest hits. She told me, "Don't give us any 'hide your light under the bushel,' or 'clanging gong' stuff. The Bible is a big book, with a lot of wisdom in it. Find some good stuff for my friends."

We talked about this concept of braking, of slowing down, of stopping. Because of her situation, she has slowed down as much as humanly possible. She's attempting to drink in the minutes with her friends, to savor the moments with her daughters. She cares about her faith, about her family, and about her friends. And honestly, that's about it. She chooses to walk bravely forward toward Jesus, holding hands with both joy and pain.

Whether or not she ever thought about slowing down before in her life, at this point she doesn't have a choice. So we talked about how to do it. "Oh, I have no idea how to do it. All I know is that life's too short," she said. "Mike, there is literally no time to keep doing stuff that steals your soul. Invest in what matters, because what doesn't matter, doesn't matter."

Before this manuscript was submitted for publication, Tamara passed away. Cancer robbed two young girls of their mom. Tamara loved her daughters fiercely, cleverly, and carefully. So I'm going to tell them something from their mom, and I'm going to let you listen in:

"Girls, your mother would want you to slow down and enjoy the ride. She would want you to stop doing anything that robs you of life. She would want you to know your life is a gift much too precious to waste. She would want you to remember that she loves you very much. And she would want you to know, when the ride of your life is over, and you hit the brakes for the last time, she'll be waiting for you at home."

14

Knowing When to Brake

He who can no longer pause to wonder and stand rapt in awe, is as good as dead; his eyes are closed.

Albert Einstein

My friend Kelly and I both got a chance to study at Pepperdine's London program. While we were there, he and I both became friends with a cool person in the program named Shana. Shana's dad was a successful musician, one of our favorites, an icon among rock legends named Van Morrison. Kelly told me that one weekend Shana invited him to one of her dad's concerts in Bath, a town in the southwest of England. He went with her, and after the concert he was invited to go with Shana backstage and meet Van and some of the other musicians. But Kelly found himself thinking that it was getting late, and he was hungry, and he really needed to grab a sandwich before he jumped the train back to London. Being backstage was nice, but there were no more sandwiches left. He was only vaguely aware of some of the hands he was shaking, so prominent in his mind had the desire for a sandwich become.

A couple of days later, Shana was talking to Kelly about the concert and said, "It was so great we got to meet Peter Gabriel and his band backstage!" Kelly looked at her blankly. Peter Gabriel was another one of his favorite musicians, but Kelly didn't remember meeting him. He had shaken his hand, but he was so focused on his hunger that it didn't even register that he was meeting another one of his favorite musicians. He needed to hit the brakes on stressing about a sandwich so he could see who he was shaking hands with. If he could have paused, he would have stood rapt in awe.

If we can't slow down the thought cycles we spin on, if we can't take a break from the urgency we constantly feel, we'll end up going through life with our eyes closed.

Since I work in a church and I know that we are always seeking to release God's people into greater ministry capacity, I know that churches consistently push people to say yes. But sometimes no is the right answer for God's greater purpose.

Take stock of the various roles you fill and the various tasks you continually sustain. Evaluate, "Is what I have said yes to still a yes?" Because some things that are values in one season of life are not priorities in another season. Maybe you're holding on to some endeavors past their usefulness in your life or your usefulness in theirs. It's like keeping fish in the fridge: while originally delicious, if you hold on too long, everything starts to stink.

Think about your life in terms of seasons. Timing is very important in the endeavors you pick up as well as when you choose to lay them down. You have to know the right decision to make, and then you have to understand the right time to make that right decision. Both are essential.

Slow Down and Enjoy

How much are we missing as we just fly through life?

One of my good friends, Tom, has a house that backs up to a small lake in a charming little corner of the world. He is an internationally acclaimed speaker and trainer who flies all over the globe, and his client list looks almost identical to the list of Forbes 500 companies. He's been in some nice places. But he told me that every morning he's home, he tries to eat breakfast looking out his back porch windows to watch what's going on at his lake. He's seen a bird of prey swoop down and pluck a trout, an otter slip across the surface of the ice on a cold winter's day, and four bucks swim across with their antlers held high, like a grove of young saplings moving steadfastly across the water.

Now, this is an important guy. He's got important stuff to do, heads of state to mentor, that kind of thing. But I'm telling you, he just sits for a bit most mornings, enjoys breakfast, and gazes out his back porch windows. And I'm also saying that he'd have missed so much beauty if he didn't have that commitment to slow down a bit.

I wonder how often God is quietly gifting us with beauty and blessing but we are running so fast that we don't even notice. When we slow down, we open ourselves up to the gifts God is leaving for us.

I'm spending a few days in a small house on Treasure Island in the Tacoma Narrows of Puget Sound. If that sounds enchanting, it is. I've got my shelter mutt horse-dog, Scout, with me, and we walk the beach together. My family came down for a day, and we explored the entire island, which is weathered, barnacled, silent like a deep sigh. We dug for razor clams at low tide and relished a huge clam feed, boiled in beer and dipped in garlic butter. A bald eagle soared in the wind right above our heads, and the vapors of this magic land thrust from the waters were filled with the cry of gull, red-breasted robin, and blue jay. Then the sun broke through the clouds of February, scattering light and glory on the Sound.

God so often meets me in solitude, in silence. He meets me in the forced hiatus from ebb and flow of pace, apart from the pulse of technology. In the quiet, I can hear the movement of a clock, the fireplace crackling, my dog stirring in his sleep. In the quiet, I can experience the presence of grace, of love's tangible arms wrapped around me. The Spirit joins me when I slow down.

Unconditional Dragon Love

My daughter, when she was three years old, loved an imaginary friend of hers. Her friend was the dragon from the movie *Sleeping Beauty*, whom she named Draggy-Drag. Alex loved Draggy-Drag fiercely. They were good friends. There were many stories told about Draggy-Drag in our family, mostly at tuck-in time, all of them very nice and pleasant. Typically the story entailed Alex riding on Draggy-Drag's willing back to go to his castle at Disneyland, which is where she met him, as a painting on the wall. She had not seen the movie, just the painting.

In the painting, that dragon is a vicious killing machine breathing deadly fire at the prince, but Alex informed us that the prince gave the dragon a glass of water, and he became nice. (I'm pretty sure this was an elaborate coping mechanism to help her deal with fear, but that's a trail for her future therapist to explore.)

Once, as a gift, she got a Disney book with the story of *Sleeping Beauty* in it, and when she opened it up to a full-page picture of the dragon, she exclaimed, "Draggy-Drag! How did *you* get here?" And we tried to explain, like the truthful parents we are, that when the book was closed, he lived at Disneyland, but the instant she opened her book, he flew to our house really fast and jumped inside the book. The dragon played a fairly significant role in our home for quite some time.

Let me assure you, there is a point to this story.

Alex drew a picture of a dragon. It was the high point of her three-year-old artistry, and she colored this dragon with great care and concern. It was really quite good, and she hung it on our fridge, telling all that this picture was for Draggy-Drag. And then, finally, Alex got another chance to go to Disneyland. She took her picture down from the fridge. She carried it with her into the park. With Alex holding the picture very carefully, we went straight to the castle, directly to the painting of the dragon on the wall, and Alex gently laid her painting down at the foot of the wall, right underneath the painting of her beloved Draggy-Drag. She left it there for him. Alex told me later that Draggy-Drag really liked his gift, that he was sleeping with it that first night. The next morning he was going to put it on his fridge.

My kid is so much cuter than your kid.

But let's get honest. Was Draggy-Drag ever going to notice? Will there ever be a draconic turning of his heart toward my daughter's affections? No. Here's the point: my daughter's love of Draggy-Drag revealed very little about the dragon, but it clearly displayed the nature of my daughter's heart. She is wonderful. Her heart loves! Her love motivated her to action on behalf of her beloved! Even when there was no response to her affection and no gratitude for her blessing, she continued her pursuit. She worked hard to love a dragon that never responded.

In this imperfect analogy, we get a glimpse into God's heart. God's heart is wonderful! God loves. He works hard to lavish beauty and kindness upon you: the extravagance of a sunset, the aroma of vanilla pine, complete and free salvation. Jesus is pouring gift after gift, blessing after blessing, upon us again and again. Whether or not we ever respond to it, God pursues us in love. Whether or not you brake long enough to notice, God blesses you. God's love for you is not influenced by you. If it was, then God would be changeable; he'd be up when you respond well, down when you don't. That reveals a needy, wimpy kind of love, bleeding in all sorts of weak, codependent ways. But that is impossible. God's love is not about you. You don't control him; none of us do. God loves you because he is love. His love is the certainty that the universe is built upon. It's what unconditional love means. He loves you perfectly because his love is perfect.

And he wants us to brake so we'll have space to notice the painting he has left for us.

How Hungry Are You?

How hungry I am determines the size of my portion.

When I was growing up, my dad had a saying at the dinner table, which I'm sure he learned as a boy. It was, "Take all you want, but eat all you take." And what he meant was that the measure of my hunger decided how much went on my plate. I wonder sometimes if that isn't the reality of our spiritual lives. God is standing at the soup pot with a ladle, and as we approach with our bowl in hand, he smiles and asks, "How hungry are you?" He turns no one away empty-handed, and the greater our appetite, the more desperate we are for what he is serving, the more our portion will be. The hungrier we are, the greater the feast.

Exodus 40:38 refers to the tangible presence of the Lord with his people, when he was visible in the pillar of fire and the pillar of cloud. And the Scripture says, "This continued throughout all their journeys." That's exactly what I pray for, that's what

I'm thankful for—that God would be so present with me that I could sense his moving; that I would be so intimate with him that I could recognize his prompting and move with him; that I would be aware of his presence throughout all of my journeys.

So contend for intimacy. Fight for it. Pause. Notice. Restructure your schedule. Repurpose your commute. Turn your thoughts into prayers. Out of intimacy with the Lord will come our authority and impact.

But this only happens as we learn when to practice slowing down, brake, and enjoy what's around us.

15

Twenty Minutes, Then Lemonade

Sometimes you need to press pause to let everything sink in.

Sebastian Vettel, champion Formula One race car driver

When I was teaching my son how to use the brakes during lesson four, it suddenly hit me like a ton of bricks: the strategic pause with Caleb was pure gold.

Each day's twenty-minute lesson ended in a break. When we parked the bike, Caleb was a victor. He would run into the house and proudly tell his mom what the lesson of the day was and how he had mastered it. That confidence encouraged him to approach the next lesson with joy and excitement. Then we'd grab a cold glass of comfort (lemonade was his beverage of choice) and just be together. It's not that we had quality conversation at that point, unless you consider Star Wars role play or nonstop sound effects "quality." It was simply our time braking together as victors.

For Caleb, there was a security in just focusing on one lesson, mastering it, and then putting the bike away while resting in the glow of success. Because each step was a baby step, he felt like a winner all the way through. So often, as parents, we try to teach our kids everything all at once, which often results in everyone being frustrated and feeling like failures, when smaller steps more easily mastered would have served their confidence and our process better. The brain dump rarely works.

This structure will help as you expand your horizon too.

A Good Coach Helps You Win

Often we're overwhelmed with the barrage of "good coaching." If you've ever gone golfing with a pro who offered to give you a few "tips," you know exactly what I'm talking about. We look at a goal, and instantly we're buried with the knowledge that there are 178 things we have to do simultaneously, and that realization is so daunting that we dive back to the couch and grab the cheese puffs.

My wife bought me one of my favorite gifts ever last Christmas, a Nikon D80 camera. With it she also gave me a book, *Photography for Dummies*. Here's the problem with that book. It made me feel like a dummy. It was huge, thick, and yellow (of course), and since it was trying to communicate multiple truths to people owning a variety of cameras, it had all sorts of diagrams and charts that included several camera makes and models. I was overwhelmed. So I left the book on the floor and went outside to play with my camera. One year later, I've taken tens of thousands of photos. That yellow book still mocks me.

God coaches us in baby steps. He instructs us gently. His yoke is light. We are not expected to be perfect in a moment. As much as I wish it would happen to me that way, it doesn't. The process that God uses takes a lifetime. We mustn't think we can master it all at once. Often the Lord will work patiently with us on one area of our character, one attitude we need to release, one part of our heart that needs healing, one circumstance we need to achieve victory in. He knows that our own journey is a series of upward movements (as well as the occasional unfortunate, downward movement). So each success is designed to buoy us up and prepare us for the next.

Every victory gets us ready to tackle the next challenge, which means that it's important to celebrate the victories and build in the pause that rejoices.

As mentioned earlier, God is the one who came up with the idea of work and rest as partners in our journey. Striving and celebration are partners. Produce, then lie fallow. Rest is actually a part of the learning, growing, strengthening process. And this is God's idea.

Picture lifting some weights. (I do this often. It's so much nicer than actually lifting them.) Even the most rigorous lifting programs will recommend that you do muscle training only four days a week, or every other day. This is because lifting tears your muscles down, literally putting tears in the tissues, and you need the break in order to heal and rebuild muscle. But equally important is that the pause allows you to conceptualize the best way to lift. After the attempt, the envisioning our minds can do is both powerful and helpful.

Downtime Clarity

I experienced this phenomenon most while learning to drive a stick shift.

My first car was that fire-engine-red 1966 Mustang my dad and I bought for five hundred bucks when I was sixteen. I loved everything about it, even the smell, which I believe was a mixture of leaded gasoline, polished chrome, and undiluted testosterone. I'd sit inside the car, as it sat inside the garage, go through another bottle of Armor All, and dream about how great it would be to get my license. I didn't have my license because I'd failed my first driving test (this still comes up in therapy), which was a problem. And I didn't know how to drive a stick shift, which was also a problem. So I asked my dad to teach me.

He did a solid job, talking me through all the steps as I watched him drive, then giving me thorough instruction as I took my turn behind the wheel. But of course I stalled, bucked, revved, ground the gears, then suddenly vaulted ahead unexpectedly. The fact that my dad didn't have a heart attack while teaching me I count as a special blessing from God (Dad agrees). After our third lesson, I was still Sir Grinds-a-Lot (also my DJ handle). So I went to my room and lay down on my bed. And then I visualized the timing of the clutch in conjunction with engaging the gears. I pictured the smooth way to depress the gas pedal. I spent the better part of the evening just resting and imagining, walking through the verbal cues my dad used to instruct me. And suddenly it all came together. I could see exactly how it was supposed to flow. The very next time I was behind the wheel, it was as Mr. Racer. Mr. Speed Racer.

But it was in rest, not work, that it clicked. It was away from the car I was desperate to drive that I finally learned.

God has often used rest to provide a real solution in my life. I'll pray over an issue and then take a run, and as I'm running God meets me with his peace. I'll wrestle over a sermon right before bed, and then in the morning the illustration is right there. God meets me with just the creative idea that was lacking. After a long, fruitless bout with an empty whiteboard, suddenly, after the creative meeting is over and you're halfway home zoning out, the ideas come flooding.

I encourage you to do the possible and trust God for the impossible. Strive hard, and then take a break. We do what we can, and then we rest.

Don't Do It This Way

My wife is coaching two of the kids' soccer teams. She's in the middle of a two-year stint as the president of the PTA at our local elementary school, and she works outside the home as a technical writer. I'm helping coach two teams as well, am involved with the board of a nonprofit organization, am a volunteer at the kids' local elementary school, and play a role in this amazing church called Overlake, which I dearly love.

So, to provide a glimpse at our madness, last Wednesday night I rushed home from the office, grabbed my son Caleb, and rushed to Duzi's soccer practice while my wife was at my daughter's soccer practice. When Duzi's practice was over, I sped home, hurriedly fed the boys and took them to Caleb's soccer practice while my daughter went to youth group and my wife went to curriculum night. After I finished soccer practice at 8:30 p.m. I rushed home, forcing the boys into showers, pajamas, and bed, while my wife did a grocery run on her way home from school. My daughter arrived home after youth group, and we hustled her through her ever-expanding bedtime practices. Around 10:00 p.m., with all the kids finally in bed and the groceries put away, my wife and I took a deep breath, gave each other a high five, and collapsed in a heap, thankful to have made it through another sprint. Then on Thursday we did it again. It's okay, because my wife and I have a free Saturday coming up here in like ten years, and we're looking forward to that time together. We're planning on napping. If we wrote a time/family/life management book, it would be called *Don't Do It This Way*.

133

Actually, Jodie and I are in a fun season right now, and we feel God's blessing over so many different aspects of our relationship and home life. I simply painted that picture to give some context for this story: last Friday evening in the midst of this busy season, Jodie was getting some things together for dinner, and she needed me to run to the store. She made me a list, and I grabbed the keys and walked out the front door. There was my daughter, Alex, on the porch. She was sitting down in the last rays of the setting sunshine, and she had her homework spread out, along with her Bible, journal, and her *Girls' Life* magazine. Suddenly it struck me that God might be offering me a moment. It felt that God had orchestrated this opportunity as a gift. And the gift was for me.

So I sat down next to her, and I began to ask her a few questions about her experience starting junior high. I asked her how she was liking it, and she told me that she was absolutely loving it. She loved the teachers, the new friends, and the sense of adventure that it provided after years in elementary school. Then she asked me, "Dad, how did you like junior high?"

"Oh, honey," I said with a smile, "they were the worst years of my life."

And I told her about how I was really popular at my elementary school in sixth grade because the big deal was playing kickball at recess, and I could kick the ball far and run fast. But in junior high all of the rules changed. Nobody cared about kickball, I wore my backpack with both straps on (a huge no-no), and it was hard for me.

We talked about her friends, her teachers, and how her classes were going. I asked her if she had seen any drugs yet, and she said, "No. Did you see drugs in junior high?" So I told her how I saw an eighth grader get arrested for selling baggies of oregano, trying to pass them off as pot (I guess he was like, "You can smoke this or sprinkle it on your pasta"), but that opened a bigger conversation about making good choices in junior high, and as we sat there in the sunshine, talking and laughing, I realized that at some point she had begun to lean against me, with her head resting on my shoulder.

It was a golden gift of pause.

Live Loved

I told my daughter I was proud of how she was living her faith and balancing life, school, and friends. I asked her if she knew that I loved her. She said, "Of course!" I asked her if she knew that God loved her, and she hesitated. Here is the struggle in her world: she feels like she has to perform to please God.

Many of us wrestle here. I know I do. I think it's one of the things that fuels the pace. It's the reason we don't like pause. It's like we don't trust Sabbath. We don't trust that God really does love us, even when we're not accomplishing something.

So I told her I wanted her to picture leaning on God's shoulder just like she was leaning on my shoulder. And I wanted her to know that God is crazy about her just like I am crazy about her. I told her that I know she's not perfect, but that she's *my* daughter, and my love covers over everything, and that's how it is with God. He knows we're not perfect, but his love through Jesus covers everything, no matter what. I said the key is to live loved. "Just live at school, loved by God. As you hang out with your friends, live loved by God. As you make your decisions, live loved by God. Live loved, and you will enjoy your relationship with God, and that will impact every other area of your life."

"Live?" I asked her, and she answered, "Loved." Her head was still on my shoulder. I took a deep breath and wished I could etch this moment forever into my frontal lobe. Suddenly my cell phone rang. It was my wife, wondering when I was going to be home from the store. I had the joy of telling her I hadn't left the porch yet.

The pause matters. The rest refreshes. Breathe. Live loved. Go hard for twenty minutes, and then go drink some lemonade.

16

Slamming on the Brakes

To have God speak to the heart is a majestic experience, an experience that people may miss if they monopolize the conversation and never pause to hear God's responses.

Charles Stanley

My friend Fergus and I were both in the sixth grade at the ice-cream social that started our final elementary school year. He had a new bike, a slick Diamondback that he won in a Little League raffle over the summer, and I coveted it. Badly. We were talking on the outdoor stage of the elementary school, which is something that I'm pretty sure they only build in Southern California. The stage was about three feet higher than the blacktop below it. Fergus was on his bike. And I was standing next to it, coveting.

Somehow in the course of our conversation I must have commented with a smile that he could probably jump pretty high on that cool new bike. Yeah, he agreed, he could. And then I think I suggested that I was sure he could do all sorts of killer wheelies and tricks on it. "I guess that's true," he consented.

"So you could probably jump right off the edge of this stage without any problems." I laid the bait out there.

"What? Off this stage?" He wasn't sure.

"Oh, come on, Ferg," I urged. "You'd rule the school," I said, hoping he wouldn't realize that as a sixth grader he already did. "I dare you." I had stopped smiling. He returned my gaze with an equally serious expression.

"You're on."

He backed up all the way to the wall, the farthest point from the edge that he could go. He began to pedal hard. He covered the length of the stage quickly. He was nearing the edge. Without question, he had enough speed to make the jump if he lifted his handlebars as he was clearing the edge. He didn't. His bike plummeted straight off the stage. He plummeted straight over his bike. I'm pretty sure the first body part to hit the blacktop was his face. It would have been funny if I wasn't equal parts afraid for his life and horrified that I had urged him to end it.

Fortunately, Fergus was okay. I mean, after the 911 call brought the ambulance that took him to the hospital and after he healed up from his concussion and his nose got back to normal. We stayed friends, but I'm pretty sure that's because he had a mild case of amnesia and couldn't remember that I was the one who dared him to vault his bike into nothingness. I suspect that Fergus's crash was single-handedly responsible for launching the California mandatory bike helmet laws.

Fergus showed me something that night. It's amazing how quickly a body stops when it slams headfirst into an immovable object.

I was wracked with guilt for months. I was afraid I would go to jail if anyone ever knew it was me who egged him on, so I never told anyone, with the exception of my dog at the time, named Beauregard, who was my silent confessor for years. Even now I'm hoping the statute of limitations has run out. I was extra nice to Fergus ever after. I slammed the brakes on instigating dangerous situations for my peers, and it was the last time I ever urged someone into a potentially life-threatening situation. I like to think it made me a better human in the long run.

Stopping Short

Slamming on the brakes always creates a disruption. It stops your ride short. Oftentimes, locking up forces a slightly sideways momentum, affectionately known as a skid-out, and one loses control, ceasing to dictate one's direction, which means that the place one ends up may or may not be where one wanted to end up. At this point in their young lives, both Duzi and Caleb want to skid the longest, so they come barreling down our hill and slam on the brakes, causing a long, curved skid to the left, which parks them neatly in our driveway with a trail of smoldering rubber evidence laid out behind them.

Even though it feels out of control, there are times when slamming on the brakes keeps you alive. There are situations where slamming on the brakes avoids the tragic accident, even though it disrupts your ride.

Seth Godin, in his book *The Dip*, debunks the old adage "Winners never quit." Winners quit all the time. Winners have actually mastered the ability to quit.

First, winners know *what* to quit. Quitting destructive habits is an incredible victory. Quitting harmful thought cycles is an enormous success. Quitting abusive relationships is liberating. Winners know to quit all sorts of things.

Second, winners know *when* to quit. When it comes to a task, a project, or an endeavor, the best time to quit is in the assessment season before you begin. That's when you count the cost of climbing the mountain, when you're determining if you've got enough energy and resources to make it to the top and back. Is the risk worth the reward? When it comes to temptation, the sooner you quit and remove yourself from temptation, the better. If you dwell in it, entertain it, and stew in it, pretty soon you're marinated in it, and it will be harder to extricate yourself from it (because where you focus is where you gravitate, remember?).

Jesus also talks about quitting. He says the time to quit is before you start. He uses the analogy of building a tower. He says don't start to build that tower unless you can finish it. If you determine you can't finish, don't start. That saves your resources as well as your reputation.

My friend Oliver realized through his premarital counseling not only that he and his fiancée did not see things eye to eye but also that it didn't concern her that they try. In most areas of life, Oliver felt, it was okay for them to be on different pages. But the issue that kept nagging him was the issue of their finances. She was tens of thousands of dollars in debt and didn't seem to care. He was one of those debt-free budget hounds, and whenever the subject of finances came up, he wasn't seeing any movement. There was no effort to get on the same page or even a recognition that marriage meant they were going to have to come up with a workable plan. He began to envision himself working tirelessly to get out of debt, only to have her unchecked spending sink them again. So he talked frankly with her about it. And she pretty much agreed that would happen. So, with two weeks to go, he called off the wedding. You might think that's hard. You're right. It is hard. It was the hardest thing Oliver has ever done. But if you're going to quit, the time to quit is before you begin.

There are some times in our lives we need to brake hard and brake now . . . like yesterday.

Slam the Brakes on Self-Harm

God made that person that you're being destructive toward when you harm yourself. And we have figured out all sorts of ways to do self-destruction. Most of us would never talk to another human with the language we use to address ourselves. If you're harming your body, your mind, or your soul, it's time to hit the brakes. I say this with no judgment, just fierce concern.

Find counseling. Seek care ministries. Pursue support groups. Connect with people who will love you, lift you up, and walk with you into a new day of self-care. These are all tools that Jesus provides in addition to the loving care of his Spirit dwelling within you. You're a temple. Treat yourself accordingly.

Slam the Brakes on Hate

The only thing God hates is sin, and the only reason he hates it is love. Yes, there is a sort of power that we mere mortals derive from hate. But we can't afford to travel on the dark side of the Force. Hate makes you hard and builds high walls around you. But at some point, you realize that the impregnable fortress you've built only serves as your prison. If you employ hate, you ultimately discover that you've sentenced yourself to solitary confinement.

When I was a junior in high school, I was wrestling my own demons of immaturity and anger, but I had some good friends who went to church, so I went to youth group with them often. That didn't stop me from being a profound idiot at school. One day, just before sixth-period English class, my friend Bill (incredulous when he found out I was frequenting church) began taunting me. "You're a *Christian*?" he sputtered in disbelief. "Yeah, right." He kept chewing on me. "Why don't you show me how good a Christian you are?"

I was furious. Understand, I wasn't sure I was a Christian. I wasn't even sure I wanted to be one. But the fact that Bill found it ridiculously impossible for me to love Jesus filled me with angry sauce. I couldn't think of anything to say. So I punched him as hard as I could in the face. Yeah, not good. Jesus is pretty clear that these sorts of angry explosions don't give him a good reputation, and they don't benefit your friendships either.

Slam the Brakes on Judgment

Are there really still people who think that some are better than others just because of the tone of their skin, their gender, their take on theology, their political affiliation? There are. Even people who are nice in many other respects are guilty of carrying insidious bias, in which they place themselves in a position of superiority. In fact, most of us are guilty of this in some regard. But heaven is going to be all kingdoms and all tribes and all tongues and every nation, and if we want to like being there, we need to practice here. If you find yourself quietly entertaining judgmental thoughts, ask for help. Intentionally build friendships across your lines of comfort. Racism and prejudice exist in every culture on earth. But God has made each one of us unique, wonderful, and in his image. We all need help remembering and celebrating the fact that we are all one in Christ.

Slam the Brakes on Blame

Somebody clever once said that you spell blame, *be-lame*, because that's what you are when you blame. And it's true, but it's worse than that. Blaming is a shield that prevents you from learning. You are protecting yourself from growth, stunting your development. When you blame, you are bypassing your own betterment. And you're the one who suffers.

Hatred, racism, and perpetual blame together effectively build a universe with you at the center. You were made for more than narcissism. The problem with pretending to be a demigod in this life is that you stand before the real God in the next one.

You need to slam the brakes on these types of mentalities, or this kind of activity, because you are causing harm. You are wounding yourself and those around you. You are accidentally wounding those dearest to you. Like secondhand smoke, you're a cancer-causing agent. Even if harm isn't your intention, you're causing it.

The first year we lived in Washington we woke up one day with our street covered in fluffy, puffy snow. Caleb was three years old at the time, and he wanted to sled down the steep street next to our house. He wanted this so much, and he was so cute begging to go. It looked a bit sketchy to Jodie and me. It was quite steep and ended at another cross street. We told him if some of the other kids were sledding on it, then maybe we'd consider, and in the meantime there was plenty of other snow play to enjoy. Later in the day, Caleb reported that there were in fact other adventurous kids sledding down the steep street. *Well, okay*, we thought, *it must not be that dangerous then.* But for some reason we couldn't take Caleb right then, so we told him we'd take him the next day.

It turned out to be really, really cold that night. Ice cold. The next morning, Caleb was up, pleading with us. So Jodie and I grabbed the plastic sled and walked with our bubbling son to the street. Everything was crispy. Slick. Smooth. The ground didn't seem to have much fluffy puff left on it. It felt harder. Icier. We slipped a few times walking to the crest of the hill. This should have acted as some sort of clue. Like I said, I was ignorant. We held the sled for our adorable son, who was brimming over with excitement. We smiled lovingly at him and then launched him, recklessly careening down the icehill of death. It turned out to be Mount Doom. He shot downhill like gravity had been handed rocket boosters. I've never seen a sled go that fast while being so out of control.

Immediately we realized what a mistake this was, so Jodie and I began to run down the hill after his wildly careening sled, but we both slipped and skidded out of control ourselves. Caleb's sled stopped immediately at the bottom, but that was because it hit a street sign. Caleb's body did not stop. He flew up and struck the street sign as well, one arm and one leg on each side of the pole, like Wile E. Coyote in a *Roadrunner* cartoon. The irony was that there was only one sign to hit on the entire street, and Caleb hit it. The only thing potentially more ironic would have been if the street sign had said, "Danger: No Sledding on the Steep Ice."

He survived, healed, flourished even, right alongside our chagrin. I still can't believe that because of our ignorance, we risked permanently damaging our son.

Here's the deal: if you keep pursuing things like hatred or blame, you're going to hurt those closest to you. If you foster racism or nurture a self-destructive streak, you'll hurt yourself, sure, but you'll end up scarring those you would die for. Maybe your excuse is ignorance (like mine was with Caleb's sledding incident). Fair enough. Up to this point, that excuse works. But if I launch my kids on another hellish ice-ageddon, I can't keep using that excuse. And now, neither can you.

Every good church in the world would love to help you slam the brakes on this stuff.

If you do find yourself stumbling into these areas (and we all stumble at various places in our lives), it's a big deal, and you need to address it seriously. God doesn't wink at your sin, but he still loves you. What I'm trying to do is get at the heart of some of the passages in Scripture where in one moment Jesus seems to take sin lightly, saying that thugs and prostitutes and tax collectors are going to be in the kingdom ahead of religious folks, and in the next Jesus seems to indicate that anger and lust are just as bad as murder and rape and need to be seriously dealt with.

Game Films

So let me try to break ground with the analogy of a sports team. Football is where my mind goes, because I had a fun high school football career: three years on varsity, inducted into the Orange County Hall of Fame for Scholar Athletes. (Does this sound like bragging? It is.) If you go back to Mission Viejo High School for their Friday night lights, you'll see on the back of the program our Hall of Famers, and on three different years you'll see the name Howerton, my brother for one year and me for two. (Can you hear those little baby tears falling? Sorry, bro.)

Fact: I didn't make every play perfectly.

Another fact: we didn't win every game.

Oh, but I wanted to! I played hard! I was intentional about learning from my mistakes. On my team we learned through game films. Have you ever watched game films? Game films might be the single most humbling invention ever known to mankind. We would show up Saturday morning after our Friday night lights and take a quick jog to loosen the bruises, and then the defensive squad would head off to one classroom and our offensive players would saunter off to another classroom, and the humble-making would begin.

We would view the game from the night before—in excruciating detail. Coach Rush would watch, rewind, watch, rewind, watch, rewind, watch, rewind, watch every single defensive play of the entire game. And God forbid if you missed a tackle, blew a read, or failed to cover your receiver. Because while it was

145

only a seven-second mistake on the game field, during films it would feel like three-day water torture.

Coach would be at the helm, watching, commenting a steady torrent of verbal judgment. "Good, good, this was a nice pursuit. Well done, Spinello. Excellent return, Jurgameyer. *Whoa!* What was that?" He'd rewind the film. "Where you going on this one, Howerton?" Rewind again. "Where in the name of holy thunder are you going?" Rewind. Coach wouldn't look at us; he'd just be looking at the film, and we'd all be watching in horrified silence. "See this, Howerton? This is the play, over here." He'd point to the side of the field that I was apparently not aware existed. Rewind. "Where in the world are you going, Howerton? Are you flirting with a cheerleader over by the sideline?" Rewind. "You do understand, the game of football is about the actual football, right? Make your read, and attack the ball." He'd be having a blast the whole time, and I'd be sliding under the desk, wishing I could disappear. I wondered if the chess team watched game films and if they maybe needed a pawn polisher.

Being Reminded of What You Already Know

Now, I don't think Jesus makes us watch game films. I think his grace erases the film.

The point is, I didn't get kicked off the team for making a mistake. The only reason to review mistakes was to try to prevent them from happening again. We didn't play every play right, and we didn't win every game, and even the games we won weren't done with perfection. But my senior year we took home the title. We were league champs. I was a contributing player on the championship team.

When it comes to our lives, with our sin, we won't get every play right. We won't win every battle. But because we are followers of Jesus, we want to battle hard. We want to slam on the brakes when necessary. We try to learn from our mistakes. And we trust that Jesus really has forgiven us, made a spot for us on his team, and won't kick us off. We trust that the cross truly is big enough to cover and cleanse and forgive all of our sins, past, present, and future. We trust that life, freedom, and healing can be our new normal. And we rejoice that we are contributing players on *the* championship team.

Lesson Five

Starting from
a Standstill

17

Starting from a Standstill

Although no one can go back and make a brand new start, anyone can start from now and make a brand new ending.

Carl Bard

When Caleb showed up for lesson five, he was exultant, Davidic, a warrior poet roaring a victory psalm. He was certain he was ox-strong. He was convinced he was a flourishing cedar. He felt vital and green. His confidence was infectious. I was happy for him and with him. I knew he would need this confidence, because I knew lesson five was a hard and final lesson in the endeavor of mastering his bike.

When we hit the driveway, we did a quick review. Caleb was nonchalant as we ran through the lessons we'd learned.

"Do you remember lesson one, buddy?"

"No fear, 'cause my dad has me." Piece of cake.

"Lesson two?"

"Balance."

"And how do you . . . ?"

"You pedal!" He was smiling. He had these nailed.

"Lesson three?"

"Steering. You avoid obstacles by looking ahead, and where you look is where you'll go."

"Lesson four?"

"Braking, which just means practicing the difference between slowing and stopping."

"Excellent. Are you ready for your final lesson?"

"Way ready, Dad."

"There is only one more lesson, and this is the final barrier preventing you from being the road warrior that you are destined to be. Lesson five is starting from a standstill."

"Starting from a standstill," he echoed.

"We could also call it starting after a fall, because you might fall now and again." I thought about my childhood friend Fergus and shuddered a bit. "No big deal though, right?"

"No big deal." He had already morphed into a road warrior.

"Caleb, this lesson is about starting using only your own strength and will. Up until this moment, I've always held the bike steady for you and provided your initial momentum. That's how you learned and practiced the other skills required. But this last lesson requires you to initiate on your own, without me bracing you to start. Does that make sense?"

"So I just have to do it all by myself? That's the lesson?" His confidence was unwavering. He was ready for this moment.

"Yup. You need to create your own momentum and on your own engage all of the skills required to ride. You know them all; you can do them all. Now you just need to put them all together. So come on. Let's take the bike to a street with some safe space."

For this lesson, we left our driveway and walked to the street one over from ours, which was long, flat, and relatively traffic free. Caleb pushed his bike and we walked together, chatting about how we couldn't wait to go for a bike ride together.

On the first attempt, Caleb fell immediately. He was unable to pedal hard enough with his right foot to get proper momentum started, so the bike circled right and he crashed quickly. Undaunted, he popped up. "I need to pedal harder," he said. He tried a second time, unsuccessfully. I watched closely to see if discouragement was going to creep in.

But the third attempt was the breakthrough. He realized that he could give himself a quick push from his standstill position in order to create the wobbling momentum he needed to get his feet in place and pedaling. I ran alongside him, celebrating his success. After a while, I asked Caleb to brake to a complete stop, in order to practice starting again from a standstill. And with this next attempt, and every attempt that followed, Caleb was a pro.

Not ten minutes later, he ran into our house and asked his mom if she wanted to ride her bike with him. She did, and the three of us rode together, praising Caleb for his technique. Like the great mom she is, Jodie gushed over her son's prowess. No other kids in the neighborhood actually rose up and called my son blessed, but if sound effects are any indication, he did imagine himself a Jedi warrior on wheels. Caleb had achieved victory in five lessons. He'd found joy and blessing through the structure of twenty minutes of hard work, and then lemonade. He had overcome.

Ready for Launch

Of course, it didn't take Caleb long before other skills were added to his repertoire, like the skill of riding without hands, or the skill of standing on his seat as he rides, or the skill of seeing exactly how long a skid mark he can leave on our driveway after he races down the hill our house is on. These are all wonderful skills that riders develop, but I didn't consider them core essentials to the bike-riding curriculum. They're electives, and most daring riders figure them out just fine on their own. After all, the skill to ride is not the actual adventure. It's just the platform from which the rider is launched into adventure.

In order to create your own momentum when starting from a standstill, you do have to believe in yourself. Now I understand that some Jesus followers don't agree that this is a value. Their view is that *we don't need to believe in ourselves; we only need to believe in God.* I readily admit that we must operate out of a healthy dependence on God's enabling power. But without a certain measure of self-confidence, we never even get on the bike.

This lesson reveals proficiency in all of the others. Starting from a standstill is the display of our mastery. We need to be able to begin again from a dead stop, because crashes happen. Chances are good that it has already happened in your life. If not, don't be surprised when it does.

Everybody Hurts

Back when my daughter, Alex, figured out how to ride her bike, I remember her crashing, hard, into the ditch near our home. That pain stole all the joy and all the motivation for bike riding right out from under her. Jodie and I were with her, and so we ran to her, picked her up, held her tight. My heart broke as her dad, because she is such a courageous, determined, tough girl, but this crash left her weeping, hurting, and fearful.

The reason my heart hurt so much for Alex was because crashing is just part of learning to ride a bike. It's an aspect of life that we will all have to deal with. Crashing will simply be part of riding the bike of life in this fallen world we journey through, whatever the endeavor. Bruce Wayne learned this from his mythic dad, who asked, "Why do we fall, Bruce? We fall so we can learn to pick ourselves up." Alex took a few moments to breathe, wiped the tears off her cheeks, and got back on the bike.

This is why creating momentum where there is none and starting again means that you've truly mastered the art. Maybe, after a particularly hard crash, you have no momentum and little motivation. You want to give up the ride. You long to have somebody else pick you up and pedal you ahead for a while. True courage is displayed right here. My dad used to say when I was growing up, "It's not a sin to get knocked down. But it is a sin to stay there."

Getting Back on the Bike

Success is how high you bounce when you hit bottom.

General George S. Patton

Of course, some crashes rock your world more than others. Some rattle your cage and leave you seeing double. I'm thinking of my buddy Jack and his young son Noah, battling hard for Noah's young life and celebrating the moments along the way, moments that have become infinitely more precious since the diagnosis. Or my friend Ethan, a hardworking and highly skilled contractor whose career was affected by the housing market crash. He has struggled for years to get solid, full-time employment again. Or my good buddy Mason who has wrestled depression for years, including a fall into darkness that nearly caused him to take his own life. You don't need any more examples to realize that crashes happen. To all of us.

And after you've dusted yourself off, caught your breath, and repaired your flat, what are you going to do? Are you going to give up? Don't do that. Remember, you've got a Father who loves you. You've got a Father who is holding you. You don't have to live in fear, because you've got a Father who can bring glory out of even the most YouTube-worthy crash.

I have a friend named Lily whose husband left her for the woman he was having an affair with. He left his church at the same time (he was a pastor) and found himself trying to get a new job, a new career, a new direction. As he did so, he discovered himself to be miserable, poor, and alone. His kids were bewildered and hurt. Lily was disoriented as well, in an indescribable amount of confusion and pain. This crash had created a lot of collateral damage. As they were beginning to walk the road of divorce, she felt a prompting from God. She wrestled with it greatly. But finally, she went to her husband and said, "Look, if you truly want out, then I'll walk that road. But if you want to reconsider, if you want to value our family again, if you want to value me again, I'm willing to begin to walk that road. Knowing that it means counseling, forgiveness, starting over in many ways—" She was interrupted by his sobs.

"Oh, thank God," he cried. "I have been such a selfish, self-centered . . . I can't even believe the guy I've become."

And she said, "You don't have to be that guy any longer." And they both started again, cautiously, after the crash.

> Though they stumble, they will never fall,
>> for the LORD holds them by the hand. (Ps. 37:24)

Bruised and Battered

> Get a bicycle. You will certainly not regret it, if you live.
>> Mark Twain, "Taming the Bicycle"

Several years ago, my brother Mark was struck by a car. He had just witnessed an accident on the freeway, so he carefully pulled his car over onto the shoulder, exited his car, and was cautiously approaching the scene of the accident. A drunk driver was speeding erratically toward the scene of the accident, saw the cars at the last moment, and swerved to avoid the damaged vehicles. But instead of swerving into the open lanes of the freeway, he swerved deep onto the shoulder, where my brother was walking, trying to help. The vehicle struck my brother, and he was catapulted over sixty feet, landing roughly in some trees.

That started a long, uphill battle of my brother fighting to restore his life. Everything was bruised and battered internally. He had multiple broken bones, including a shattered femur. Even when the leg healed, it healed one and a half inches shorter than his other leg. So over a year later, the surgeons ended up removing an inch and a half from his undamaged femur, so both legs would be the same length.

Through no fault of his own, my brother experienced a horrific crash. And he learned, painful step by painful step in physical therapy, how to courageously start again from a standstill. Honestly, he is one of my heroes. He overcame.

God met him along the way, with healing, with humor, and with courage. Ten years later, Mark is healthy, energetically athletic, the father of four amazing kids, and husband to an incredible lady, my kids' aunt Kristen. He runs his own counseling firm, kayaks in the waters off Newport Beach, and never complains about the inch and a half he lost. He used to be six foot three. Now he's six foot one and a half. If that happened to me, I'd be a hobbit. As it is, I'm still wondering why they couldn't transfer that inch and a half to these two femurs of mine.

Every single one of us must start from a standstill. It will reveal our mastery. Because crashes happen. And when they do, we bounce.

18

Bounce

If you live long enough, you'll make mistakes. But if you learn
from them, you'll be a better person. It's how you handle ad-
versity, not how it affects you. The main thing is never quit,
never quit, never quit.

former President William J. Clinton

On March 10, 2012, Levi Leipheimer crashed three times in a
single leg of the Tour de France. The *Velo News* article about
it stated: "Three crashes in the penultimate stage of Paris-Nice
saw Levi Leipheimer tumble out of contention for the overall
when he was just 10 seconds out of the lead."[1] The first crash
was his own fault, when he dropped his jacket and it got caught
in his front tire. The second happened on a downhill stretch
when another cyclist clipped him from behind. And the third
time, his team had gathered around him and they were closing
in on the peloton (the main group of cyclists in a race), when
they rounded a corner on the descent and collided with a police

motorcycle that had been unfortunately parked on the wrong side of a turn. Four out of five of his teammates went down in a tangle, including Leipheimer:

> "I think we set a record for the number of crashes on the Col de Vence," sport director Brian Holm said. "That's racing. It's too bad, because with just 10 seconds behind Wiggins, I am pretty sure Levi could have won tomorrow."[2]

Crashing is always a bummer. A fall always produces frustration. Occasionally it prevents a specific win that you had your sights set on. But, as Brian Holm pointed out, that's racing.

You're never exactly ready for a crash either. Nobody is really prepared. That's why it's called an accident. A biker on my street who is in great shape, who hosts his own bike races, was trucking downhill on a trail near our home one twilight last summer, and as he was gaining speed a deer darted in front of his bike. They collided, head over hoof. The man broke his collarbone and his bike's front fork, but the deer just went, "What the bleep was that?" and ran off.

Jesus knows of our capacity for crashing. He knows all of the ways we fall. He knows it more intimately than we can understand, because what he did on the cross was acknowledge your sin, all your brokenness, and take it upon himself. He did this for all of us. He took every rape and every murder, every enslaving oppression and every hate-filled scream. He took all of our interpersonal warfare and all of our inner personal junk. Jesus took each shame-filled moment we've chosen for ourselves, and he pulled it into himself, and it was nailed to the cross with him. He knew exactly how much we needed forgiveness, and so he paid for our forgiveness with his life. And even as he took the darkness onto himself, he prayed: "Father, forgive them, for they don't know what they are doing" (Luke 23:34). Just when we've experienced the most painful crash available, Jesus is there to wrap us up in his arms of grace, to pick us up in love, and to help us get back on the bike.

A few years ago, because of addiction and brokenness, Brent and Mindi got divorced. Since then these two friends of mine have pursued Jesus, sobriety, and wholeness in our Celebrate Recovery ministry. Along this journey, they watched as their friendship began to flourish again. Romance was rekindled. Last Tuesday night, they got married again, for the second time, to each other. As a part of their ceremony, they nailed their old divorce papers to the cross. Then I stood to pray a blessing on them, and my voice was thick with emotion. I told them that might be the clearest picture of the good news of God's unfailing love that I had ever seen. I'm the one who keeps running away from God, who keeps crashing in the ditch, who keeps handing him my divorce papers. And he keeps on loving me. He takes those divorce papers and nails them to the cross.

We can bounce after a fall because grace is based upon God's character, not our crashes. It's measured by God's infinite capacity, not our finitude. The grace of Jesus doesn't depend on me. As humans, we are arrogant and egocentric by nature, and we think that his grace must be based upon our performance. Listen: God doesn't reject believers when they sin, because salvation isn't based on human accomplishment.

God doesn't reject me when I fall, because his love is unconditional, everlasting, never-ending, and my salvation isn't based on my performance. It is based on God and his desire to shower my life with mercy. His mercies, by the way, are new every morning.

The situation we find ourselves in, after experiencing God's forgiving grace, is that we still crash from time to time. We still find ourselves in the midst of a struggle, and this struggle can cause us to despair. Paul was an apostle, specifically writing to the many churches that he started in his travels. He was an amazing Jesus follower with a testimony of moving from murderer to minister, and some may be tempted to call him a super Christian (faster than a speeding heresy, able to leap tall Bible concordances in a single bound). But in his letters, Paul gives us some insight into his own dependence upon God's grace. His confession is that he does what he hates, and he hates what he does. He knows what falling three times in one race looks like. Yet he knows that the love of God is more overwhelming than any crash. He learned that grace is sufficient. Because of the grace Jesus offers, Paul bounced. And so can we. (See Romans 7:14–25 and 2 Corinthians 12:7–10.)

True Grit

> Who ever said anybody has a right to give up?
>
> Marian Wright Edelman, activist and
> founder of Children's Defense Fund

When she was teaching in the inner city, Angela Lee Duckworth discovered that IQ was not the best determinant between her highest and lowest performing students. There was another quotient that consistently turned up in her best achievers, and since she didn't know exactly what to call it, she named this quality *grit*. Duckworth went on to graduate school to become a psychologist in order to study education from a motivational perspective. She and her team wanted an answer to the question, "Who is successful here and why?"

They began rigorous research in multiple fields. From West Point to the National Spelling Bee to the Chicago Public Schools, they found the same formula: success was largely determined by *grit*. By steadfast perseverance and stamina. By looking toward the future, day in and day out. By working intentionally to make that future a reality. And by understanding that momentary failure is not a permanent reality. Duckworth confessed that she didn't know how to increase grit in students. So her challenge was that we must become gritty about making our students grittier.

I suggest we need to encourage one another to bounce.

> The godly may trip seven times, but they will get up
> again.
> But one disaster is enough to overthrow the wicked.
> (Prov. 24:16)

The righteous fall seven times, but they rise again. They bounce. They get moving again and bless God for the seven-fold tenacity that comes from having the power of the living Jesus inside. In trying to launch the new venture, have you stumbled? In attempting the new intimacy with Jesus, have you faltered? In striving to balance some areas of your life, have you crashed? Is there a place in your life in which you've steered yourself into a ditch?

Get back on, get moving, and embrace the power of God in a new day. Start again from a standstill. Remember, bodies at rest tend to stay at rest. A body in motion tends to stay in motion. Defy inertia, and get back on. It's time to bounce.

I know a woman who bounced and is now living seventeen years sober after addiction had tanked her life and relation-ships. I know a man who bounced and in humble love reached out to his estranged daughter after twenty-seven years of si-lence. I know a husband and wife who left their successful careers to care for disabled children in a country where ser-vices for disabled people are nonexistent. I know a man who found Christ in prison, bounced, and now leads a ministry to inmates. There are hundreds upon thousands of stories of how, through faith in Jesus and grit, we can bounce again after a fall.

Emerging from a Cocoon

For Christmas, the kids had received a butterfly atrium, so Jodie sent away for some mail-order caterpillars, and before long we received five. Each of us named one, and Cindy, Charles, Petunia, Meister, and Dingus fascinated the Howertons daily. We watched them crawl, eat, and grow. We were mesmerized when they planted themselves and spun the mummy bags that they crashed in for a while.

Our band traveled through the pupae stage successfully. They each wove their chrysalis successfully. Each one wormed its way out of the cocoon successfully. Their emergence is a beautiful image of starting from a standstill.

But even though they were fluttering around in their indoor mini-atrium, when we released them into the wild they balked. On a sunny afternoon, we set them free, but they didn't fly. Our butterflies didn't fly. They were butterflops. They clung to blades of grass, had their backs arched, and were staring upward into the big blue. Duzi was down close staring at them intently, and then he turned and looked straight up, wondering if they were seeing something up there that we were missing.

The lifespan of the Pink Lady Butterfly is only a few weeks long, so each moment they waited was like months off of their lives. I was terrified they were wasting the short time they had left. But they just stood still, clinging. I willed them to flutter. I spoke to them compellingly. "Come on! You were made to *fly!*" And then it hit me: that's where God finds me. The next morning, journaling my thoughts to God, I wrote:

Lord, in how many ways am I like one of those butterflies? Not living the life, the passion, the design, the creative uniqueness that you have in mind for me? Please allow me to be filled with your Spirit and to walk in your truth. Please allow my vessel to be cleansed and filled completely with your radiant light and life.

Please make me forever discontent to cling to blades of grass.
Please find me ready to spread my wings and soar.

The next day we went out, and all five were still there. The sun was out, and as it warmed, they opened and closed their wings slowly. When they were all warmed up, they fluttered off into the rest of the adventure that God had for them as transformed creatures. That's my prayer for me, and that's my prayer for you. By God's grace, by his Spirit, he has transformed us into winged creatures.

We can't afford to allow a crash to keep us down. We can't afford to waste a single minute clinging to blades of grass. Not now, not ever. Cooperate with his work by stretching your wings and flying. Let's bounce.

Get Back On and Get Moving

Your present circumstances don't determine where you can go; they merely determine where you start.

Nido Qubein

Starting from a standstill is the true test of mastery. In life, this gets tested when we start along a new path. When we pull up our tent stakes and travel to a new circumstance, this is where we are challenged most severely.

I was a pastor serving at a church called Saddleback Church in Lake Forest, California, which is a great church. I have wonderful friends there, and I invested six years of my life in ministry there. I was shown a model for big faith and radical obedience. I planned to spend the rest of my life there in the sunny Southern California surf with ministry thriving, family nearby, and close friends. Yet in spite of how perfect everything seemed, I felt God stirring some divine discontentment in my heart. I began to pay attention and pray about it but had no clue what to make of it.

When Overlake Christian Church called from the east side of Seattle, I was not interested. I imagine this was exactly how Jonah responded when the word of the Lord came to him. ("Nineveh? No thanks." The line goes dead.) I enjoy just a handful of things that I was not interested in giving up, like sunshine. Overlake's executive pastor, Dana, posed the question, "Mike, what would stir your passion?" And the more I dared to verbalize some dreams, the more excited he became on the other end of the line. Turns out, the church leaders had the same dreams. Still, we had no immediate plans to pack it up. After all, I had just joined the LA Fitness that opened up across from my church. Bad time to move.

Overlake wanted me to visit, and so Jodie and I agreed to come. We communicated on the front end that we were 99.9 percent sure the answer was no. I just wanted the guys at Overlake to invest their money in a candidate that was actually looking for a job. We were not looking and not really open to the possibility of God's call. We'd come up for a weekend away, but we were thinking *no way*. (I'd heard that to get to the nearest surf you had to drive three hours for "shark-infested-frigid-cold-you've-got-to-be-kidding-my-eyeballs-are-frozen" kind of waves. Not interested.)

When we arrived, the sun was out. It was May in Seattle, and when the sun is shining it rivals Eden. It's a masterpiece. Exquisite. Trees, mountains, the bluest sky you've ever seen. And Starbucks' (the drive-through kind, just like we'll have in heaven) mermaidian logo winked at us from every corner. We walked on the church campus for the first time. I got chills, and not from the cold. (The sun was out, remember? Just like it is nineteen other glorious days a year.) I talked to leaders and members of the congregation all weekend. I talked to pastors.

God was prompting me to see that there was more potential in that platform for the gospel of Jesus Christ than in any place I'd been in my entire life.

How could this be? I had just received some great affirmation from Saddleback's pastor, Rick Warren (in the form of a kind raise, which is nicely tangible affirmation), and I had a 401(k) going and a safe plan of surfing weekly and growing old and leathery and whitening my teeth like everyone else in Orange County, and then this. *What are you doing to me, God? You can't possibly be calling me away from this!*

We dreamed. We listened. We decided. It was evident that God was moving something in our hearts and in our friends as we shared what was going on with our small group. So I think it was a bit of a surprise to everyone when I called Overlake up in Seattle and told them no. The truth was that I was afraid. I didn't believe that God was my heavenly Father and that he had me. So it took me a while.

I spent another year pedaling, doing fulfilling ministry at Saddleback Church. Crave (the college age ministry I worked with) was legitimately fun. Lives were being changed! Our college ministry was growing from 90 students toward 600. I published two book projects, and they sold *dozens* (mostly to my extended family—my mom loved them, and my aunt Kay. My wife was aware I wrote them.). I was working with an alternative service on Sunday evenings that had grown from 250 to nearly 1,800.

But there was this nagging suspicion that God was calling me to Seattle.

Good Things versus God's Best

My boss, friend, and mentor, Doug Fields, once told me that if you're emotionally healthy and you are cranking in ministry and there's still that dream that you can't get out of your mind, that's God tugging on you. I'm not sure how emotionally healthy I was (or am), but I definitely was beginning to see that God was haunting me with Seattle. It was a dream from God to steer my life by. Rick Warren wrote me a note at this same time and reminded me that even good things aren't God's best if they aren't the good things that God is calling you to.

So a year later Jodie and I made the move to Seattle (the Promised Land for heliophobes—those who fear sunlight) to take a spot on the team at Overlake Christian Church. We started a service called Illuminate and developed a leadership crew, and over eighteen months we saw the thing grow from forty toward two thousand, from one to four services on a weekend. We were underfunded, but God had begun to do a good work.

While we were launching these services, we had staff meetings in our home and interns living with us, and like all movements of God, it was messy. We were literally exhausting ourselves for the sake of the gospel. When it came to living in balance, we weren't. We weren't doing the best job of pacing ourselves, of stewarding our relationships with our spouse, with our kids, and, more important, with our hearts.

Not everyone at Overlake was excited about Illuminate's trajectory. As growth happened, we began feeling more and more uncomfortable. Every week we wanted to celebrate something good, but we couldn't, because it would unfortunately be seen as a negative by some on our church staff, and feelings would be wounded. Our legitimate celebrations of what God was accomplishing through knuckleheads like us were viewed by some as knuckleheaded crowing. And as much as I wanted to be a humble leader in God's movement, I know that pride was constantly flirting for my attention. Part of my personal challenge in this season was that I needed to look up from the day-to-day pace and chaos of ministry to the longer view of where we were going. We were hurtling at breakneck speed down a long, treacherous hill, and it was becoming apparent that none of us was steering. And nobody had the slightest idea how to brake.

Comparison was a killer, and honest conversation needed to happen. Our Illuminate services were maxed out, especially at our 11:00 a.m. service, which was our service with the most seekers and the most faith decisions made. We were nearing a crisis point. I was sensing that our church needed to be unified, as were other pastors on the team. Though we were personally *for* each other, the bulk of the tension seemed to exist between my supervising pastor and me. Instead of alternate services that were complementary to the whole, things had become competitive.

Driving into a Ditch

A change was inevitable. It felt like we were merrily barreling toward a train wreck. I was certain that we needed to brake for a while, to take a look ahead, to begin to steer in a new direction with balance and pacing, and to pursue unity. But I was afraid, because I felt there was a chance the whole thing could blow up, and I'd be the one responsible for the crash.

Since I believed sincerely that God had called me to OCC, I was truly confused. I could tell that we were nearing the edge of something. This was a feeling shared by several, although I don't think any of us knew what to do about it. Did we trust that God truly had us? Were we willing to become balanced in our approach to life and ministry, to our values and purposes? Did we have a clear vision of where we were steering? Would we be committed to learning how to brake? The answer to all of these questions was no.

All I knew was that our work scenario felt like pedaling a beach cruiser through a hurricane. Tensions were high. Conversations were strained. Everyone was polite and kind on the surface, and it was obvious that all of the pastors and elders really did love each other, and that we all loved Jesus. But there was dysfunction in our family. And in the midst of the confusion, I crashed. Hard.

The supervising pastor called a team meeting and laid some ground rules: "We have a problem and we need to talk honestly about it. What are the elephants in the room—the things that nobody is talking about but that we must address?"

In a healthy team environment, this is one of the best questions you can ask as a leader, because you really want to deal with the things that everyone is thinking but nobody is saying. In a team environment that isn't so healthy, this is simply a question you don't answer. If only I had Proverbs 21:23 memorized then, which says, "Watch your tongue and keep your mouth shut, and you will stay out of trouble."

Either I was dumb or proud (I imagine I was both), but I answered the question. Honestly. I addressed some of the real issues that we needed to talk about, beginning with our need for unity. I tried to be respectful and careful. I tried to affirm as I critiqued. I sought to have a critical mind without having a critical heart. I pitched a plan or two that I thought might bring us together as a church body. I was neither perfect nor brilliant, but I thought things were going well.

Right up to the moment I got fired.

20

Starting Over

Success is the ability to go from one failure to another with no loss of enthusiasm.

Sir Winston Churchill

Being terminated felt like an uppercut that landed just underneath my right rib cage, bruising my liver. I couldn't breathe. That time when my daughter was learning to ride her bike, she came barreling around the corner, lost control, and flew furiously into a deep ditch. Her wail of pain came from a place of deep surprise and wounding. That's the same silent wail that was thunderously echoing in my own head.

Here's what was so confusing: I thought I was here to help. I thought I had heard God stir this dream in my heart. I was certain I had heard God say, "Steer this direction. Travel along this road." Great things were happening in ministry, in individual hearts. I was pedaling my hardest but wasn't entirely balanced. And I hadn't looked ahead down the road for a long time. Suddenly I realized that I was the one responsible for this crash. And it was more painful than I had ever anticipated.

My wife called me to ask how the meeting went. "It went fine," I think I said.

"Oh?"

"I've been terminated," I think I said.

Silence.

"I'll see you at home," I think I said.

"Are you okay, baby?" she asked.

"I think so," I think I said.

It is hard to describe how I was processing the event. I don't even think it was computing. Being fired had fried my emotional wiring. I was the kid in school who never got in trouble. Every job I've held I've moved ahead in. Teachers have always affirmed me. Bosses have honored me. So I had very little frame of reference for what I was going through. I'm a bit of a people pleaser; I'd never been off-roading like this before, stuck in the brush, bike upended, wheels lazily spinning.

Unsure of how to proceed, I lived in that ditch.

I wasn't allowed to come to my office. I wasn't allowed to check my email. I didn't have access to my computer. I think there was some fear that I would make waves, which I understand, but it still felt like salt in my wounds. I asked my administrative assistant to gather some personal things from my office for me. I kind of hovered around coffee shops, a genial haunting, like Casper the moody ghost. Those were dark days. Crashing can be a dark and lonely prospect. I had wrestled with God on the front end of relocating to Seattle and had done it largely in faith that God was my Father and that he wouldn't let me fall. But now the whole thing had fallen apart. How was I supposed to feel now?

Part of what I felt was freedom. Free, like a skydiver feels free, only I wasn't wearing any sort of parachute. My stomach was in knots. I had no money in savings and no job opportunities lined up, but I felt absolutely that God was with me, holding me, whispering words of his call on my life. Once again, without any expectation that it was possible in the midst of this pain, I heard God again. And once again, what I heard him say was simple: "You can trust me. You really can." So I decided to believe this, no matter what. I chose to accept lesson one, that my Father had me.

So with Psalm 120:1, which says, "I took my troubles to the LORD; I cried out to him, and he answered my prayer," and the Lord's reminder that I could trust him, the troubled cry of my prayer went like this:

Lord God Almighty,
This feels like the most painful crash I can imagine. I want to thank you for loving me. Thank you for hearing me, for knowing me, for holding me, for forgiving me, for saving me. Jesus, these steps you have me walking are new, exciting, adventurous, frightening, and absolutely exhilarating. I am so thankful for your presence, your movement, your power, and your light. I'm thankful that you lead me. I'm thankful that whatever happens from here happens with you first. Thank you for your shelter in the midst of the storm. Thank you for catching me in this fall. Please help me to get back up and start the journey again. Amen.

Starting Again from a Standstill

Being fired isn't good for anyone's resume. And it happened right when I was trying to correct our lack of balance, our breakneck speed, and the absence of any steering mechanism. So I spent some days getting on my face before Jesus, surrendering to him, saying, *God, I thought you called me to this. I thought you steered me here. I thought you wanted these dreams for me. But Jesus, I see how my immaturity and pride have come into this. I see how difficult this road is with my impatience mucking things up. I also see how being humble is not just one of many options right now. It's my only option.*

I decided to humbly get back on the bike.

I had an incredible resource in a few key friendships. This is my personal testimony to why it is essential for every human being to develop intimate spiritual relationships with a few safe and trusted friends. These were dear friends who loved me but who weren't impressed by me. I was gifted with a group of brothers and sisters who cared for me deeply. Their friendship carried me.

I had my family. They were like a foundation for me. When the world seemed to sway and buckle, one of my sons would climb up on my lap and ask me to read his Hardy Boys book to him. My daughter would tackle and tickle me. My wife would simply sidle up next to me and squeeze my hand. These were tangible encouragements for me, meeting me in the ditch I had landed in.

And I had Jesus. I've heard people talk about how it was in the midst of the crash that Jesus kept them sane, held them close, that the presence of Jesus was palpable throughout the crisis. That Jesus was the one picking them up, dusting them off, telling them he had more in store for their journey. I believe them. That was my experience. Once my numbness wore off, I realized that it was Jesus caring for me, it was Jesus ministering to me, it was Jesus who was loving me as I'd never allowed him to because I always had everything handled.

And what I found was that I could accept his invitation to trust him. I kept driving by the church, lovesick (but couldn't stop in, remember?). I felt like a junior higher listening to '80s tunes on his Walkman, riding his Huffy past his ex-girlfriend's house, wishing he had the courage to ring the doorbell.

I drove home.

Losing my job was the hardest crash I've ever experienced. And I know that I'm not alone in walking this kind of road. Even as I write these words, I have friends who have been living with the trauma of job uncertainty in a troubled economy for quite some time. Some seasons are extremely difficult, and you simply wonder, *Where is Jesus in the midst of all of this?*

He's running right behind your seat, whispering, "I've got you. I've got you." And he does.

It was an eternal two weeks after being fired that I found myself sitting at the table with the elders and my supervising pastor. I was respectful and honest. I didn't fight for my job. I simply submitted to the elders and to the leadership of my boss. But the pie I was eating was entirely humble. My pride was being killed. I chose to walk a road of complete surrender, trusting that Jesus was all I needed and that he had planned a way out of this mess. And at that time I was reinstated as a pastor on Overlake's senior associate team.

Later that day I got alone with my boss and asked him if it was supposed to feel like this, if it was supposed to feel like a death. "Yeah," he said. "That's how it feels." He was on his own journey through this, and I count him an honorable man God has given me as a true friend and mentor. Sometimes brothers in ministry must go through seasons like this, for the growth of all involved. Just ask the apostle Paul and his traveling companion John Mark.

These two followers of Jesus had a disagreement that was so sharp they parted company (Acts 15:36–41). But Paul took Silas, and Barnabas teamed up with John Mark, and the gospel was spread twice as fast. John Mark wrote the Gospel according to Mark, and Paul penned roughly three-quarters of the New Testament. Not a bad multiplication. And at the end of Paul's life and ministry, we see him writing to John Mark, his true friend when others had deserted him, greatly desiring his companionship (2 Tim. 4:11). Mere mortals really can work through conflict and continue to make a difference for the kingdom. But it feels like hell sometimes.

As it turns out, God was going to use this crash to launch both my supervising pastor and I on a new adventure. But right then we were both still reeling from the pain of landing in the ditch.

New Horizons

It's been quite a ride. The ride of my life. Less than a year after being reinstated, I was prayed over by the elders of our church and commissioned as the lead pastor. My former boss has started an overseas leadership training ministry; he splits his time between Jerusalem and Seattle, and he and I remain friends to this day.

As I jumped into my new role, I realized I had no idea what to do as lead pastor. Fear began to take hold again. I sensed God inviting me to trust him and to seek the advice of others who had been there before me. So I grabbed two pastors (Pastors Sonny and Gib, with over forty years of ministry experience each), and I called a few other young lead pastors with no experience. In other words, I sought out wisdom and experience, as well as pastors who were clueless but committed. I have eternal gratitude for Pastors Scott, Mark, Jud, Ryan, and Grant.

On my first day as the lead pastor, I sensed that the only way to start out an endeavor like this is on one's knees, so I hit my knees first, confessing everything I could think of—every thought, every word, every action, every limitation, every good thing that falls short of God's best thing. (I have to do this often, by the way.) And I invited the elders to join me. Then I invited the staff to join the elders and me, and then I invited the congregation to join the staff and the elders and me. Thousands of us, on our knees before God Almighty, asking him to move in his church, asking him to forgive our boneheadedness and to use even amateur bikers like us for his glory. And he has. The ride has been amazing.

Seven years later, we're profoundly enjoying God's presence and blessing. We're seeking to walk with him and without fear. We're trying to pedal hard and live with balance. We're striving to look ahead and to go along the path that God leads us on. We routinely hit the brakes on things that are no longer helpful for the journey, and we occasionally slow things down just to take in the view. And even if we tumble or crash along the trail, we pick ourselves up, dust ourselves off, and ask Jesus for the grace to cover our mistakes and for the energy to begin again.

When it comes to so many in Scripture (think of Joseph, the Israelites in Egypt, David, Jonah, Daniel, Jesus, Peter, Paul, and just about everybody else), the road to God's victory led through places dark, deep, and depressing. When it comes to my story, I'd say the same thing. I'd bet the same is true with your story. But the darker the road, the brighter the triumph. And you can never tell what desperate place God will bring you through, with your humble obedience, revealing his glory and victory in a unique way. God often chooses roads that are entirely unexpected:

> Your road led through the sea,
>   your pathway through the mighty waters—
>   a pathway no one knew was there! (Ps. 77:19)

No one can see the whole path ahead. That's why we must continually choose to ride along our road obeying God with great joy. Because he knows who we are and what we need. He knows where we are. And he knows where we're going. So journey with him.

He sees the whole road.

Conclusion

Every day you may make progress. Every step may be fruitful.
Yet there will stretch out before you an ever-lengthening, ever-
ascending, ever-improving path. You know you will never get
to the end of the journey. But this, so far from discouraging,
only adds to the joy and glory of the climb.

Sir Winston Churchill

In the summer of 1975, immediately following his high school
graduation, my buddy Scott and his friend Shawn got on their
bicycles. From Seattle they caught the ferry across Puget Sound
to Bremerton and kept riding south. That night, over a hundred
miles later, they camped out above Longview, on the banks of
the Columbia River.

"Are we really doing this?" Scott asked his friend.

"I think we are," Shawn replied.

For the next two months, they biked the highways and by-
ways of these western United States. They traveled south into
California, east into Nevada, and then north all the way up to
Coeur d'Alene, Idaho. They became saddle sore. At one point,
Shawn got clipped by a semi and went tumbling down the

gravel shoulder off the road. He survived. They both developed Herculean calf muscles. They recovered. That trip became a golden memory that Scott would celebrate for the rest of his life and a powerful encouragement for him to live fearlessly in other areas of his life as well.

The point of learning to ride is never learning to ride. The point of learning to ride is the adventure that it launches you on.

Once Caleb mastered these five lessons, the world was our oyster. We'd ride down the Pipeline Trail to the main road, up past Cottage Lake to the grocery store, where we'd grab an ice-cream treat before heading home. Just today we were riding down the hill from our house, and he did the whole thing without hands, wearing my full-face motorcycle helmet, because that's how eleven-year-olds roll.

Can you remember that thrill of learning to ride? Do you remember the adventure and freedom that learning these lessons brought? Incredible, right? New horizons opened up to you. Glorious vistas were now within your reach. Adventure was in the palm of your hand and life on the edge of your banana seat.

I want to conclude with a series of questions:

What are you doing, right now, that compares even slightly to that feeling?

Where are you challenging yourself?

Where are you learning a new skill?

Mastering a new technique?

Finding a new hobby?

Seeking healing and wholeness in the areas where you need it? Enriching your current skill set?

Expanding your career?

Finding new ways to communicate age-old truths?

Who are you loving outlandishly?

What are you learning to ride, right now?

God has an amazing purpose for your life, and part of his purpose is that you would learn, expand, grow, overcome. This is not for our own inflation or arrogance. The fourth chapter of the book of Revelation reminds us that we receive our crowns from the Lord only that we might lay them before his throne. We must spend our lives going deeper with him, maximizing our impact, bettering ourselves, and sucking the marrow out of life. This is not only for our best; ultimately, it's all for his glory. He gets our crowns, thankfully received, joyfully offered.

I grew up watching the Jetsons, which means I have always wanted a flying car that folds up into a briefcase. I have been captivated by a company called Terrafugia (in Latin it means "escape Earth") that designs and builds airplanes with retractable wings. You could park the thing in your garage, drive to the gas station to fill up, then extend the wings and take a day trip to Niagara Falls.

One interesting thing about this company is that it began as a dream for some students at MIT. They were obsessed with the idea of a practical flying car. They dreamed, and designed, and organized, and fund-raised, and finally they had the know-how and the financial backing to make their company a reality. Now they had to move from imagination to actuality. They had to build a prototype. I imagine that for years the prevailing question was, "Can we make it fly? Can we make it fly? Can we make it fly?" And they've done it. In March of 2009, the Terrafugia Transition took its first successful flight. This roadable aircraft can fly. Now the only question that remains is, "Where shall we go?"

Learning to ride a bike is only the beginning. Mastering a new skill is just the introduction. Learning a new language, beginning a new relationship, charting a new course—these things are only the means. They begin the journey. They launch the adventure. Where is yours leading you?

It's time to jump in. Call the girl. Plan the trip. Ask the question. Book the lesson. Buy the guitar. Begin by walking. Appreciate the small things. Notice the blessing. I want to challenge you to tune into God's Spirit and listen to his promptings. He's the one who has an adventure in store for you. I encourage you to breathe deeply the breath of God.

It's time to declare: I want to tell a great story with my life, and I want it to be the story that the Lord is guiding me into. As you tune into God's Spirit, ask him: "What is the new adventure you are guiding me on? What do you want to do in my life? With my life? What is the next horizon that you want me to explore?" Whatever it is, these lessons will work for you.

Have no fear. Why? Because your heavenly Father has you.

Live balanced. How do you balance? Pedal.

Steer well. You go where you're looking. Your direction determines your destination.

Brake often. Learn how to slow, and know when to stop.

And if you do fall, dust yourself off, get back up, and give it another go, because crashing is simply a part of riding. You can do it. I know you can. You'll be glad you did. And once you do it, you'll never forget how to do it again. Abundant life is at stake. God's glory is ready to be revealed through you.

Each one of us is wired differently. We all have different starting places, different roads we walk, different strengths and weaknesses. The abundant life is not about comparing yourself to another person to see if you have got more tally marks than they do on some achievement checklist. Abundant life is about fulfilling the unique call God has for you. It's about facing every challenge in your pathway with fearless energy and true grit. It's about keeping your eyes on the horizon with passion and joy—knowing that there are obstacles, knowing that circumstances will need to be overcome, knowing that as you look up the mountain from the base of the foothill you will be tempted to conclude, "This is impossible." Now you're equipped for the challenge, of course, because you know without a doubt: nothing is impossible with God.

One of the things that both Jodie and I heard from God when we decided to steer our lives up to Washington from California was the phrase, "You can trust me." Multiple times I felt that God was gently and lovingly holding me with that phrase, "Mike, you can trust me."

When I was going through my dark season, I felt that was the case again, that God was there, in the midst of uncertainty, in the midst of fear, of being out of balance, of not being able to see ahead, of having fallen, hard. I wasn't sure of hardly anything, but I was sure God was there once more, saying yet again to my heart, "Mike, you can trust me."

During the roller-coaster ride that was our adoption story, so many times our heart was in our throats. There were tears and anxiety and all manner of midnight prayers heaved skyward as we ended up hitting a dead end two separate times. And even then, when we felt afraid, like our dream to adopt Duzi might be crushed by international bureaucracy, our Father was there again, whispering, "Mike, you can trust me."

And so I did. And I found what so many have found—that you can trust him. He's got you. He'll steady you and will never let you go. He knows the exact way your life needs to balance, the deep healing you need. The Lord knows the path he is leading you on and the direction he wants you to go. Trust him to help you steer.

Jesus knows where you need to slow and precisely what you need to stop. And when you fall, the Lord will pick you up, take care of you, and gently get you moving again. You can, and you will bounce back after a crash. This is why you can fearlessly embrace your next adventure. His perfect love casts out all fear.

As you carefully and calmly walk these steps, your universe will be expanded. You will overcome. You'll go places you only dreamed of going. And you'll do things, accomplish goals, touch hearts, change lives, and reveal the kingdom. You'll make an impact in your world by embracing your new horizon. The new "bike" God is prompting you to "ride"—it's for your best and for his glory.

So it's time. What are you waiting for? Pick your bike back up out of the shrubs. Use a clothespin to clip the ace of hearts to your spokes. Kick your leg up over that banana seat. Start the journey.

It's time to take the ride of your life.

A Note to My Children

It has to be a weird deal to have a pastor dad who writes sermons and books filled with anecdotes about how you learned to ride a bike, the South African accent you used to have, and the imaginary dragon you played with when you were three. So to my children, Alexandra, Caleb, Duzi, this book is also dedicated to you. My gut tells me, however, that you won't read my writing until you're older and I'm dead. So if that is the case, and it's a long time hence, and if at some point in your future you find yourself bored on a rainy Sunday afternoon, and you pick up this book, or any book of mine, and begin to read it, my gentle prayer is that you find the stuff winsome, loving, and not overly exploitive. My prayer is that it points you to the heart of Jesus, the most winsome and loving heart there is. I am sincerely humbled by you. My heart overflows with love for you. You make the journey extraordinary.

This book is what happens above the surface of the waters. But there is a greater love, a moving joy, a more vibrant life just below the surface. And I live primarily frustrated, sensing that I lack the word-craft, the subtlety of thought, the spiritual capacity to draw these deeper things from the water out into the warm sun. But I can point, I can shout, I can call people over and say, "Look! Look! There! Do you see? Just there! That movement in the waters! That's what I've been trying to say!" And a crowd gathers and strains to see, looking this way and that way, into the murk.

Meanwhile, quietly, Jesus motions me over. He invites me to drift away from the crowd, grab a snorkel, and slip over the edge of the dock. He invites me to submerge, with him, into the depths of God's goodness.

He invites you as well.

I sure hope you take him up on it.

I want them to be encouraged and knit together by strong ties of love. I want them to have complete confidence that they understand God's mysterious plan, which is Christ himself. In him lie hidden all the treasures of wisdom and knowledge. (Col. 2:2–3)

About the Author

(in His Own Words)

I've been a pastor for over twenty years, meaning that my "credentials" are almost exclusively from church world, which can be a bizarre sort of place. I received my graduate degree from Fuller Theological Seminary and studied philosophy and literature at Pepperdine (facts people systematically refuse to be impressed by). I've served over thirty thousand clients (aka congregants) in four different ministry seasons, each of which have been glorious messes (the settings, the congregants, and their pastor). I'm currently serving as the lead pastor of a church that, based on size, budget, and productivity, is in the top half of 1 percent of the roughly four hundred thousand churches in the United States. This is even more impressive considering that I have sincere desire and affection for Jesus but feet of clay that stumble continually (when they're not firmly planted in my mouth).

I've been involved in starting initiatives from scratch that have grown from a few dozen folks to thousands, and I've transitioned established ministry settings from traditional to modern, from lethargic to progressive. And here's the hard, honest truth: outside of church world, these accomplishments are as pointless as windshield wipers in Tucson. If you're a normal human (that is, not a pastor), then this bragging is as foolish as a sprinkler system in Seattle. Nobody cares. In fact, I'll bet that none of that gets me as much leverage in your world as this simple feat: I taught all three of my kids to ride a bike.

Well, my wife and I did. And God.

And we're still riding.

Notes

Lesson Two Balance

1. Dave Ramsey, "The Seven Baby Steps," DaveRamsey.com, 2014, http://www.daveramsey.com/new/baby-steps/.

Lesson Five Starting from a Standstill

1. Andrew Hood, "Leipheimer Crashes out of Contention at Paris-Nice," VeloNews.com, March 10, 2012, http://velonews.competitor.com/2012/03/news/leipheimer-crashes-out-of-contention-at-paris-nice_208910.
2. Ibid.

Mike Howerton is lead pastor of Overlake Christian Church in Redmond, Washington, and served for six years as the college pastor at Saddleback Church. He is a graduate of Pepperdine University and received his master's degree from Fuller Theological Seminary. Mike is the author of *Glorious Mess* and lives in Washington with his wife, Jodie, and their three children.

Also by
MIKE HOWERTON

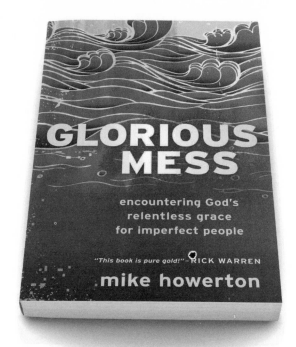

In **Glorious Mess**, Mike Howerton clearly reveals God's perfect love for imperfect people. Includes insightful discussion questions for group or personal use.

Visit GLORIOUSMESS.ORG